KB004966

TALK TO ME IN KOREAN
LEVEL 6

*Have More Engaging Conversations
by Expressing Doubts, Abilities, and Happenings*

This book is based on a series of published lessons, divided into ten levels, which are currently available at https://talktomeinkorean.com.

TALK TO ME IN KOREAN
- LEVEL 6 -

Talk To Me In Korean - Level 6

1판 1쇄 • 1st edition published		2018. 11. 12.
1판 8쇄 • 8th edition published		2024. 7. 22.

지은이 • Written by		Talk To Me In Korean
책임편집 • Edited by		선경화 Kyung-hwa Sun, 에밀리 프리즈러키 Emily Przylucki
디자인 • Designed by		선윤아 Yoona Sun
삽화 • Illustrations by		김경해 Kyounghae Kim
녹음 • Voice Recordings by		선현우 Hyunwoo Sun, 최경은 Kyeong-eun Choi
펴낸곳 • Published by		롱테일북스 Longtail Books
펴낸이 • Publisher		이수영 Su Young Lee
편집 • Copy-edited by		김보경 Florence Kim
주소 • Address		04033 서울특별시 마포구 양화로 113, 3층(서교동, 순흥빌딩)
		3rd Floor, 113 Yanghwa-ro, Mapo-gu, Seoul, KOREA
이메일 • E-mail		TTMIK@longtailbooks.co.kr
ISBN		979-11-86701-09-6 14710

*이 교재의 내용을 사전 허가 없이 전재하거나 복제할 경우 법적인 제재를 받게 됨을 알려 드립니다.

*잘못된 책은 구입하신 서점이나 본사에서 교환해 드립니다.

*정가는 표지에 표시되어 있습니다.

Copyright © 2018 Talk To Me In Korean

*All rights reserved. Partial or in full copies of this book are strictly prohibited unless consent or permission is given by the publisher.

*Defective copies of this book may be exchanged at participating bookstores or directly from the publisher.

*The standard price of this book is printed on the back cover above the UPC barcode.

TTMIK - TALK TO ME IN KOREAN

MESSAGE
FROM
THE AUTHOR

We are at Level 6 already! At this level, you are already familiar with most of the fundamental Korean sentence structures and grammar rules. With this grammar textbook, however, you will learn how to make your Korean sentences even more specific and detailed by adding extra elements to them and emphasizing certain parts.

As you must be well aware by now, the key to improving your Korean even more from now on is by practicing a lot. You can also try to express the same idea in various new ways instead of just sticking to the expressions with which you are comfortable. The chapters in this book will help you learn new tools that you can use in forming new types of Korean sentences.

We hope you enjoy learning with this book and improving your Korean sentence-building skills even further. Thank you very much for studying with Talk To Me In Korean and also, congratulations on your determination to continue learning! 이 책도 여러분에게 많은 도움이 되었으면 좋겠습니다. 앞으로도 저희 톡투미인코리안 교재들로 즐겁게 공부해 주세요!

TABLE OF CONTENTS

LESSON 1

How about …?

어때요?

Track 01

In this lesson, let us take a look at how to say "How about...?" in Korean. There are many ways to say this, but the most basic and common way is, "어때요?".

How about...?

= Noun + 어때요?

Ex)

사과 어때요? = How about an apple?

커피 어때요? = How about some coffee?

= Verb stem + -는 거 어때요?

Ex)

먹다 + -는 거 어때요? → 먹는 거 어때요? = How about eating?

보다 + -는 거 어때요? → 보는 거 어때요? = How about watching?

어때요? comes from the verb 어떻다, which literally means "to be how". Therefore, when you want to say phrases such as, "How about this one?", "How about that one?", "How about eating here?", etc., you can use the verb 어떻다.

When speaking with friends, you can use 반말 and drop the 요 at the end.

> **Ex)**
> 어때? = How is it?
> 이거 어때? = How about this?
> 커피 어때? = How about some coffee?

Examples with Nouns

Track 01

1. 이거 어때요? = How about this?

2. 생일 선물로 카메라 어때요? = How about a camera for your/his/their birthday present?

3. 내일 어때요? = How about tomorrow?

Examples with Verbs

1. 다시 하는 거 어때요? = How about doing it again?

2. 다른 사람한테* 물어보는 거 어때요? = How about asking other people?
   * *If you want to say "to" other people, you have to add the particle, -한테. -한테 indicates that you are asking those people a question and not asking about those people.*

> **Ex)**
> 주연 씨한테 물어보는 거 어때요? = How about asking Jooyeon?

3. 안으로 들어가는 거 어때요? = How about going inside?

Sample Sentences

이거 싫어요? 이거(는) 어때요?

= You do not like this? How about this one?

* "이거 어때요?" is the plain form. Therefore, you can add the topic marker 는 when you are comparing a number of items and have already asked the person, "How about this one?".

내일 만나서 이야기하는 거 어때요?

= How about meeting and talking about it tomorrow?

이렇게 하는 거 어때요?

= How about doing it this way?

* You can say this when you want to make a suggestion while doing something or trying to solve a problem. It can almost be interchangeable with, "I have an idea!"

Track
01

Word Contractions

When you want to make a verb into a noun, you add -는 거. The original form is -는 것.

-는 거 + Subject Marker (이/가) → -는 것 + 이 → -는 것이 → -는 게
-는 거 + Topic Marker (은/는) → -는 거 + 는 → -는 건

이렇게 하는 거 어때요? [Neutral]

= How about doing it this way?

이렇게 하는 게 어때요? [+ Subject Marker]

= How about doing it this way?

   * *The meaning is almost the same as the neutral sentence.*

이렇게 하는 건 어때요? [+ Topic Marker]

= (Since you are not too sure about the other ideas,) How about doing it THIS way (then)?

If you want to ask in the past tense you can say:

어땠어요? = How was it?

**Track
01**

by Expressing Doubts, Abilities, and Happenings

Sample Dialogue

🎙
Track
02

현우: 경화 씨, 점심 뭐 먹고 싶어요?

경화: 비빔밥 어때요?

현우: 비빔밥 좋아요. 아는 식당 있어요?

Hyunwoo: Kyung-hwa, what do you want to eat for lunch?

Kyung-hwa: How about bibimbap?

Hyunwoo: Bibimbap sounds good. Do you know of a place?

🖊 *Exercises for Lesson 1*

Make a sentence by combining the phrases and translate them into English.

1. 이거 + 어때요? →

    =

2. 내일 + 어때요? →

    =

3. 다시 하다 + -는 거 어때요? →

    =

4. 내일 만나서 이야기하다 + -는 거 어때요? →

    =

Rewrite the following sentences after shortening the parts that can be contracted, and then translate them into English.

5. 이렇게 하는 것이 어때요? →

    =

6. 이렇게 하는 것은 어때요? →

    =

Check the answers on **p.208**

13

LESSON 2

What do you think about ...?

어떻게 생각해요? / 어떤 것 같아요?

Track 03

In this lesson, let us take a look at how to say "What do you think about...?" in Korean. In our previous lesson, we introduced the expression 어때요?, which means "How about...?". Sometimes this expression, 어때요?, can also be used to mean, "What do you think?".

어때요?

= How is it?

= How about...?

= What do you think?

When you want to add more details to the sentence and say, "What do you think about + Noun?" or "What do you think about + Verb-ing?", you need to use different expressions.

There are various ways to say, "What do you think?" in Korean, so let us take a look at the two most commonly used expressions.

14

1. 어떻게 생각해요?
= What do you think?

어떻게 = how, in what manner
생각하다 = to think

2. 어떤 것 같아요?
= What do you think?

것 같아요 = I think, you think

> **Ex)**
> 좋은 것 같아요 = I think it is good.
> 큰 것 같아요 = I think it is big.
> 비 오는 것 같아요 = I think it is raining.

Track 03

The word "what" is used for the English translation because you ask "what" is on someone's mind or "what" are their thoughts about a certain topic, but in Korean, you use the word "how" because you are asking about "how" someone looks at the matter or "how" they think something is.

The basic verb for "to be how" is 어떻다 and when you change it into an adverb, it becomes 어떻게.

어떻게 생각해요? is literally translated as "HOW think?"

어떤 것 같아요? is literally translated as, "HOW it seems?" or "What kind of thing it seems like?" (*To review -(으/느)ㄴ 것 같다, go back to Level 3 Lesson 9.*)

15

Koreans frequently use, "어떻게 생각해요?" in both written and spoken language, but "어떤 것 같아요?" is used more often in spoken language.

What do you think ABOUT + Noun?

The expression for "about" in Korean is -에 대해서. -에 means "to/at/toward", and 대해서 means "about".

about school = 학교에 대해서

about me = 저에 대해서 (formal language), 나에 대해서 (casual language)

about what = 뭐에 대해서

You can add -요 at the end to make a complete sentence: "뭐에 대해서요?" Sometimes, people also drop the 서 at the end and just say -에 대해.

Track 03

What do you think about _____?

= _____에 대해서 어떻게 생각해요?

= _____ 어떤 것 같아요?

> **Ex)**
>
> What do you think of the school?
>
> = 학교에 대해서 어떻게 생각해요?
>
> = 학교 어떤 것 같아요?

What do you think ABOUT + Verb-ing?

In order to use "about / -에 대해서" after a verb, the verb needs to be changed to the noun form of -는 것.

하다 = to do

16

하는 것 = noun of 하다

이렇게 하다 = to do it like this
→ **이렇게 하는 것에 대해서** = about doing it this way

물어보다 = to ask
→ **물어보는 것에 대해서** = about asking

Ex)
물어보는 것에 대해서 어떻게 생각해요?
물어보는 것 어떤 것 같아요?

To make this expression easier to pronounce, you can drop the ㅅ consonant in 것에.

Track 03

물어보는 거에 대해서 어떻게 생각해요?
물어보는 거 어떤 것 같아요?

Sample Sentences

이 책에 대해서 어떻게 생각해요?

= What do you think about this book?

이 책 어떤 것 같아요?

= What do you think about this book?

* Remember, if you use 어떤 것 같아요 you do not need to add the word "about/-에 대해서" because 어떤 것 같아요 already means, "What does it seem like?".
** 어떤 것 같아요 is more commonly used with friends or those you are close with.

17

어릴 때 유학을 가는 것에 대해서 어떻게 생각해요?

= What do you think about studying abroad at a young age?

어릴 때 유학 가는 거, 어떤 것 같아요?

= What do you think about studying abroad at a young age?

제 아이디어에 대해서 어떻게 생각해요?

= What do you think about my idea?

제 아이디어 어떤 것 같아요?

= What do you think about my idea?

Track 03

* In English, you can ask someone what they thought in the past tense, such as, "What did you think about my idea?", but in Korean, you do not say, "제 아이디어에 대해서 어떻게 생각했어요?" because if you say it in the past tense, it usually implies the person changed their mind.

** You can also say, "어떻게 생각하세요?" if you would like to sound more polite or formal.

Sample Dialogue

Track 04

효린: 주연이 결혼식 때 이 옷 입고 갈까?
　　　어떻게 생각해?

민희: 너무 화려하지 않아?

효린: 그럼 이건 어떤 것 같아?

민희: 오! 그게 훨씬 낫다.

Hyorin: Should I wear this to Jooyeon's wedding?
　　　　What do you think?

Minhee: Isn't it a bit too colorful?

Hyorin: Then, what do you think about this?

Minhee: Oh! That's much better.

by Expressing Doubts, Abilities, and Happenings

✎ Exercises for Lesson **2**

Rewrite the sentences using **어떤 것 같아요?**

1. 학교에 대해서 어떻게 생각해요?

(   )

2. 물어보는 것에 대해서 어떻게 생각해요?

(   )

3. 이 책에 대해서 어떻게 생각하세요?

(   )

4. 어릴 때 유학 가는 것에 대해서 어떻게 생각하세요?

(   )

5. 제 아이디어에 대해서 어떻게 생각하세요?

(   )

Check the answers on **p.208**

LESSON 3

One of the most …

가장 ... 중의 하나

In this lesson, let's take a look at how to say "one of the most..." in Korean. After studying with this lesson, you will be able to say things such as, "He is one of my closest friends", "It is one of the most popular places in Seoul", etc.

Now before we talk about how to say this in Korean, we would like to point out that this expression actually came into widespread use as a result of Korean people being exposed to the English language. At first there were some who tried not to use this expression because it sounded too much like a "translated" sentence, but now it is so commonly used that not many people actually care.

One of the most... = 가장 ... 중의 하나

First of all, let's break down the phrase word by word.

21

One = 하나

of = -의

* 의 is pronounced as 에[e] in spoken Korean. Even though it is easier to pronounce it this way when speaking, you should write 의 and not 에, like it sounds.

the = It is not translated into Korean in this case.

* The word order for this phrase is different than in English, plus the word "the" is not used since you do not need it in Korean. You only need it when you want to specify "that person" or "that one" and would use 그.

most + Adjective + Noun = 가장 + Adjective + Noun

* If you would like to review 가장 (= most), go back to Level 4 Lesson 18.

1. Word order difference between Korean and English for "-의 / of"

In Korean, -의 is the particle that shows possession, belonging, origin, or characteristics, and it basically means "of". The word order, however, is very different for -의 or "of" in these two languages. If you say "A of B", in Korean you need to switch it to "B의 A". To make it simpler, you can just think of -의 as **'s**, as in "my friend's house", "my teacher's name", etc.

It is the same for the expression in this lesson; in English, the word "one" comes at the beginning, but in Korean, "하나 (= one)" comes at the end.

2. 하나 can be replaced by other words

하나 is the most basic form of saying "one" but depending what you are counting, you can use different counting units. Let's take a look at some of the most commonly used ones.

Person = 한 사람, 한 명, or 한 분 (honorific)

Place = 한 곳, 한 군데

Thing, Kind, Type = 한 가지

Go back to Level 2 Lesson 9 to review the lesson on counters.

If you want to stick to the most neutral expression, you can use 하나.

3. To understand how to use 가장 with adjectives or verbs, there are three lessons that you need to have studied.

- Level 4 Lesson 18 (on how to say "best" or "most" using the superlatives 가장 and 제일)
- Level 3 Lesson 13 + 14 (on how to make adjectives out of descriptive and action verbs in Korean)

🎙️
**Track
05**

Examples:

가장 + 예쁘다 → 가장 예쁜

가장 + 좋다 → 가장 좋은

가장 + 괜찮다 → 가장 괜찮은

   * 괜찮다 originally means "to be okay" but it can also be used to mean "to be good".

가장 + 친하다 → 가장 친한

   * 친하다 means "to be close with someone" or "to be close friends".

You should always include a noun as it does not make sense to only use a verb.

가장 예쁜 친구 = the prettiest friend

가장 좋은 책 = the best book

가장 괜찮은 카페 = the best café

23

가장 친한 친구 = the best friend

4. How to use 중 as "among" or "of"

중 literally means "middle" or "center", but when used after a noun and followed by -의, it means "among" or "(one) of (the...)".

Noun (plural or singular) + 중

Examples:

가장 예쁜 친구 = the prettiest friend

가장 예쁜 친구들 = the prettiest friends

among my prettiest friends = 가장 예쁜 친구들 중(의) = 가장 예쁜 친구 중(의)

one of my prettiest friends = 가장 예쁜 친구들 중의 하나 = 가장 예쁜 친구 중의 하나
(You can even drop "의" and just say "가장 예쁜 친구 중 하나".)

method/solution = 방법

the best method = 가장 좋은 방법

the best methods = 가장 좋은 방법들

among the best methods = 가장 좋은 방법들 중(의) = 가장 좋은 방법 중(의)

one of the best methods = 가장 좋은 방법들 중의 하나 = 가장 좋은 방법 중의 하나
(You can even drop 의 and just say 가장 좋은 방법 중 하나.)

Now let us look at some examples of the entire structure.

24

가장 ... 중의 하나

가장 좋은 웹사이트들 중의 하나
= 가장 좋은 웹사이트 중의 하나
= 가장 좋은 웹사이트 중 하나
= one of the best websites

가장 빠른 길들 중의 하나
= 가장 빠른 길 중의 하나
= 가장 빠른 길 중 하나
= one of the fastest ways/paths

Track 05

가장 자주 만나는 친구들 중의 한 명
= 가장 자주 만나는 친구 중의 한 명
= 가장 자주 만나는 친구 중 한 명
= one of the friends that I meet most often

* Note that you cannot always drop whatever word you want in Korean. However, you can do it if the phrase is commonly used and can still be understood. If you use the word 하나, you are talking about many things and then picking just one of them, so you do not need the plural suffix -들.

Sample Sentences
여기가 제가 제일 자주 오는 카페 중(의) 하나예요.
= This is one of the cafés that I visit most often.
    * Since "café" is a place, you can change 하나 to 한 곳/한 군데.

by Expressing Doubts, Abilities, and Happenings

Ex) 여기가 제가 제일 자주 오는 카페 중의 한 곳이에요.

** In spoken Korean, 제일 is used more often but in written Korean, use 가장.

제가 가장 좋아하는 가수들 중(의) 한 명이에요.

= He/She is one of my favorite singers.

= He/She is one of the singers I like the most.

한국에서 가장 인기 있는 영화 중(의) 하나예요.

= It is one of the most popular movies in Korea.

Track 05

Sample Dialogue

 Track 06

석진: 저는 박사 과정 포기해야 할 것 같아요.

현우: 왜요?

석진: 여러 가지 이유가 있는데, 가장 큰 이유 중의 하나는 높은 등록금이에요.

Seokjin: I think I have to give up on my PhD.

Hyunwoo: Why?

Seokjin: There are many reasons, but one of the biggest reasons is the high tuition.

✏️ Exercises for Lesson **3**

Fill in the blanks by unscrambling the words in the parentheses.

Check the answers on **p.208**

1. 중 빠른 하나 길 가장

(   ) = one of the fastest ways/paths

2. 친구 가장 중 명 한 만나는 자주

(   ) = one of the friends that I meet most often

3. 가수들 중 가장 한 명 좋아하는

제가 (   )이에요. = He/She is one of the singers I like the most.

4. 카페 하나 자주 제일 중 오는

여기가 제가 (   )예요. = This is one of the cafés that I visit most often.

5. 인기 중 하나 있는 영화 가장

한국에서 (   )예요. = It is one of the most popular movies in Korea.

28

LESSON 4

Do you mind if I ...?

-아/어/여도 돼요?, -아/어/여도 될까요?

In this lesson, let's take a look at how to ask someone if they would mind if you did something, or if it is okay to do something.

Track 07

In order to say this in Korean, you can use structures -아/어/여도 되다 and -아/어/여도 괜찮다 (you can go back to Level 4 Lesson 8 to review how to use -아/어/여도 되다). Therefore, you literally say, "Is it okay if I...?" or "Is it okay for me to...?".

Let's look at the various ways of saying this in Korean.

1. Verb stem + -아/어/여도 돼요?

This is the simplest structure. The verb 되다 here means "to be okay", "to be doable", or "to be possible" and -아/어/여도 means "even if..." or "even when". So all together, -아/어/여도 되다 means "to be okay (even) if...".

29

Sample Sentences

여기 앉아도 돼요?

= Do you mind if I sit here?

옆에 앉아도 돼요?

= Do you mind if I sit next to you?

창문 닫아도 돼요?

= Do you mind if I close the window?

창문 열어도 돼요?

= Do you mind if I open the window?

Track 07

나중에 전화해도 돼요?

= Do you mind if I call you later?

2. Verb stem + -아/어/여도 괜찮아요?

This is almost the same structure as -아/어/여도 되다, except the verb here is 괜찮다. These two structures are interchangeable, but -아/어/여도 괜찮아요 has a slightly softer nuance, whereas -아/어/여도 돼요 tends to be a little more direct. By using -아/어/여도 괜찮아요, you give the other person an impression that you are being more careful. You can use this with people who are older than you or with someone you do not know.

Sample Sentences

저 먼저 가도 괜찮아요?

= Do you mind if I leave first (before other people)?

30

여기 앉아도 괜찮아요?

= May I sit here?

이거 열어 봐도 괜찮아요?

= Do you mind if I open this? / or Do you mind if I try opening this?

내일 말해 줘도 괜찮아요?

= Do you mind if I tell you tomorrow?

> * "내일 말해 줘도 돼요?" is more direct. "내일 말해 줄게요." is even more direct.

3. Verb stem + -아/어/여도 될까요?

This structure uses the verb 되다 again, but here it is used in the -(으)ㄹ까요 form, which we introduced in Level 3 Lesson 4. By using -(으)ㄹ까요, you can express your curiosity or uncertainty about something, therefore naturally asking for the other person's response or feedback. Asking 될까요? makes your sentence softer and more polite than simply saying 돼요?

Sample Sentences

여기 앉아도 될까요?

= Do you mind if I sit here?

= Would you mind if I sit here?

= I wonder if I can sit here? (You are not directly asking the other person, but more asking yourself.)

창문 닫아도 될까요?

= Do you mind if I close the window?

= Could I close the window?

나중에 전화해도 될까요?

= Do you mind if I call you later?

= Can I call you later?

4. Verb stem + -아/어/여 주실래요?

With all three structures above, you can express, "Do you mind if I...?" by asking the other person if it would be okay if YOU did something. However, if you want to ask THE OTHER PERSON whether he or she would mind doing something, you can use the structure -아/어/여 주실래요?.

주다 means "to give", but when you combine it with other verbs, -아/어/여 주다 means "to do something for someone", and the honorific suffix -시- makes your sentence more polite.

Track 07

Sample Sentences

조금 기다려 주실래요?

= Do you mind waiting for a bit?

    * In casual language, you can say 조금 기다려 줄래?

한 번 더 설명해 주실래요?

= Do you mind explaining one more time?

    * In casual language, you can say 한 번 더 설명해 줄래?

Keeping the same kind of nuance, you can change the sentence ending to the following:

(I) -아/어/여 주실래요? → -아/어/여 줄래요?

(줄래요? is a little less formal than 주실래요? without the suffix -시-.)

(2) -아/어/여 주실래요? → -아/어/여 주시겠어요?

(주시겠어요? is interchangeable with 주실래요? but a little more polite and formal.)

by Expressing Doubts, Abilities, and Happenings

Sample Dialogue

Track
08

종업원: 지금 빈 테이블이 없네요. 조금만
　　　　기다려 주시겠어요?

손님: 네. 잠깐 나갔다가 와도 될까요?

종업원: 네. 그럼 여기 전화번호 적어 주세요.
　　　　빈자리 나면 전화 드릴게요.

*Employee: We currently do not have any empty
tables. Would you mind waiting just a
bit?*

*Customer: Sure. Do you mind if I go somewhere
and come back in a moment?*

*Employee: Okay. Please write your phone number
here. We will call you if a table opens
up.*

✏ Exercises for Lesson 4

Write three different phrases to ask permission for each situation.

1. You would like to ask someone if it would be okay if you sit here.

-
-
-

2. You would like to ask someone if it would be okay if you close the window.

-
-
-

3. You would like to ask someone if it would be okay if you call him/her later.

-
-
-

4. You would like to ask someone if it would be okay if you leave first.

-
-
-

5. You would like to ask someone if it would be okay if you try opening this.

-
-
-

Check the answers on **p.208**

by Expressing Doubts, Abilities, and Happenings

LESSON 5

I am in the middle of -ing

-고 있는 중이에요, -는 중이에요

Track 09

In this lesson, let's learn how to say that you are "in the middle of doing" something in Korean. In Level 2 Lesson 10, we introduced the structure -고 있다 as the plain present progressive, and now let's take a look at some other ways of expressing the present progressive by using the word 중.

중 = middle, center, medium

The word 중 can be used with many other words to form various meanings that are related to middle, center, or medium.

Ex)
중학교 = middle school
중간고사 = midterm exam
중앙 = central

When you want to say, "I am in the middle of doing something", you can use 중 in the form

36

of -고 있는 중이다.

-고 있는 중이다 = to be in the middle of + Verb-ing

The basic form of the present progressive is -고 있다.

Ex)
먹고 있다 = I am eating.
뭐 먹고 있어요? = What are you eating?

You can add the ending -는 to change the verb into an adjective to modify the noun 중 .

-고 있 (progressive) + -는 중 (in the middle of Verb-ing)
-고 있는 중 + -이다 (to be)
-고 있는 중이다 (to be in the middle of Verb-ing)

Track 09

You only conjugate the verb -이다 at the end to express the tense of the sentence.

Ex)
Present: -고 있는 중이에요.
Past: -고 있는 중이었어요.
Future: -고 있는 중일 거예요.

Sample Sentences
가고 있는 중이에요.
= I am on my way.
= I am in the middle of going.

* You can say "가고 있어요" to mean the same thing, but -는 중 emphasizes the fact that you are doing something right at this very moment.

뭐 하고 있는 중이었어요?
= What were you doing?
= What were you in the middle of doing?

열쇠를 찾고 있는 중이었어요.
= I was in the middle of looking for the key.

* For all the sentences above, you can change -고 있는 중 to -는 중 to mean the same thing.

Track 09

가고 있는 중이에요. → 가는 중이에요.
뭐 하고 있는 중이에요? → 뭐 하는 중이에요?
열쇠를 찾고 있는 중이었어요. → 열쇠를 찾는 중이었어요.

Sample Mini Dialogues

1.
A: 공부해요! 언제 공부할 거예요? = Study! When are you going to study?
B: *하는 중이에요! = I am!

* You can say 하는 중이에요 in other forms as well.
Ex)
하고 있어요.
하고 있는 중이에요.

If you are upset, you can add -잖아요.

Ex)

하는 중이잖아요.

2.

A: 뭐 하는 중이었어요? = What were you doing?

B: 아무것도 안 했어요. = I did not do anything.

3.

A: 다 샀어요? = Did you buy everything?

B: 아직 고르는 중이에요. = I am still in the middle of choosing.

Track 09

Sample Dialogue

🎙
Track
10

경화: 석진 씨, 집에 도착했어요?

석진: 아니요. 지금 다시 회사로 가는 중이에요.

경화: 네? 왜요?

석진: 지갑을 놓고 왔어요.

Kyung-hwa: Seokjin, did you get home?

Seokjin: No. I'm on my way back to the office.

Kyung-hwa: What? Why?

Seokjin: I left my wallet there.

✏️ Exercises for Lesson 5

Rewrite the sentences by adding -는 중 *to emphasize the fact that you are doing something right at this very moment.*

1. 가고 있어요.　　→

2. 뭐 하고 있어요?　　→

3. 뭐 하고 있었어요?　　→

4. 열쇠를 찾고 있었어요.　　→

5. 아직 고르고 있어요.　　→

Check the answers on **p.208**

41

LESSON 6

Word Builder 9

-님

Track 11

Word Builder lessons are designed to help you understand how to expand your vocabulary by learning and understanding some common and basic building blocks of Korean words. The words and letters introduced through Word Builder lessons are not necessarily all Chinese characters, or 한자. Though many of them are based on Chinese characters, the meanings can be different from modern-day Chinese. Your goal through these lessons is to understand how words are formed and then remember the keywords in Korean to expand your Korean vocabulary from there. You certainly do not have to memorize the Hanja characters, but if you want to, feel free!

In this lesson, we are looking at a native Korean suffix, -님.

The word 님 basically has the same goal as 씨, which is to show respect to the person being addressed or mentioned, but 님 is much more formal and polite than 씨, and therefore it is used very commonly with formal social titles.

You can use 님 after a person's name when addressing him or her in the most formal way.

42

For example, if your acquaintance's name is 현우, and you are speaking casual language with him, you can just say the name alone - 현우. If you want to be more polite and formal, you add -씨 after the name and say 현우 씨. But if you want to be even more formal, you can use 님 instead and say 현우 님.

Sometimes on the Internet, people who do not know each other but still want to be formal will just use the word 님. This is mostly only common among young people.

The following are some of the most commonly used words in Korean in which you can find the suffix -님. Many of these words are FIXED, which means they can NOT be used WITHOUT the suffix -님; some of them CAN be used without -님, but the nuance will change.

Track 11

1. 선생님 = teacher
* Almost always used with -님 attached. If you only say 선생, you may sound disrespectful. 선생님 is used both when you address a teacher directly and when you talk about a teacher when he or she is not present.

2. 장님 = a blind person
* Some people think it is more appropriate to use the term 시각 장애인 (visually handicapped person), but the word 장님 is still commonly used and you can NOT use the word without -님 attached.

3. 의사 선생님 = doctor
* The job itself is 의사 but when you address and talk to a doctor, you cannot call him/her 의사. You need to use the word 의사 선생님. If you are a doctor, you would say "저는 의사 예요. (I am a doctor.)" because you do not show respect to yourself.

4. 교수님 = professor

* The job itself is 교수 but when you talk to a professor, you need to put the suffix -님 and call that person "Name + 교수님" or just 교수님.

5. 어머님 = mother

* You can call your own mother 엄마 or 어머니 if you want to be more polite, but when you refer to someone else's mother in a polite way, you use the word 어머님. It is not natural, however, to use the term 어머님 to talk about your own mother to someone else. In that case, 저희 어머니, "my mother", is better.

6. 아버님 = father

* The same with 어머님. You can call your own father 아빠 or 아버지, but when you refer to someone else's father in a polite way, you use the word 아버님. When you get married, you should call your wife/husband's father, 아버님 and mother, 어머님.

Track 11

7. 형님 and 누님 = older brother and sister (for a man)

* When men address an older man, they use the term 형, but when they want to be very polite (not necessarily "formal" in this case), they attach the suffix -님 at the end. The same goes for 누나, a term for men to use to address an older female, except 누나 changes to 누님 instead of 누나님.

8. 손님 = guest

* In the past, the sino-Korean word 손 could be used on its own to mean "a guest", but in modern-day Korean, the suffix -님 is ALWAYS attached at the end of the word. In a more business-related context, you can call your customers 고객님. In the case of the word 고객님, it is OKAY to drop -님 when you are NOT addressing a person directly.

More Examples of Job Titles

9. 사장님 = head of company + -님

10. 과장님 = section chief + -님

11. 부장님 = head of department (or manager) + -님

12. 총장님 = dean or president of a college + -님

Track 11

Sample Dialogue

Track
12

민송 엄마: 선생님, 안녕하세요. 저 민송이
엄마예요.

선생님: 민송이 어머님, 안녕하세요.

민송 엄마: 민송이가 감기에 걸려서 지금
병원이에요. 오늘 유치원에 10
시까지 가도 될까요?

선생님: 네, 괜찮아요. 이따 봬요.

Minsong's Mom: Hello. I'm Minsong's mother.

Teacher: Hello, ma'am.

Minsong's mom: Minsong has a cold so we're
at the doctor's office. Would it be
alright if we got there by 10?

Teacher: Yes, that's fine. See you later.

✏️ Exercises for Lesson 6

Respond to the following questions in Korean.

1. "Doctor" who treats people who are ill is 의사 in Korean. How do Koreans usually address the doctor when they call them?

....

2. "Professor" who teaches at a university or college is 교수 in Korean. How do Korean students address them?

....

3. What is the Korean word that means customer, visitor, or guest?

....

4. How do Koreans call someone else's mother in a polite way?

....

Check the answers on **p.208**

by Expressing Doubts, Abilities, and Happenings

LESSON 7

One way or another

어차피

Track 13

In this lesson, let's take a look at the Korean expression 어차피. 어차피 can mean many things in English; it does not translate very well. In most cases, it is used as part of a sentence, but it can be used on its own very often as well.

Various translations of 어차피:

- anyway
- one way or another
- not even... to begin with
- in any case
- after all

The basic meaning of 어차피 is "whether you choose this or choose that" or "no matter what choice you make". You use 어차피 when you have an expected result in your mind or to show your skepticism for someone's worries or expectations.

The multiple usages of 어차피 can be best explained through examples.

48

Examples

I. 다시 올 거예요.

= I will come back.

= I will come again.

= They/He/She will come again.

→ 어차피 다시 올 거예요.

= I will come back anyway. (So don't worry if I forget something. I can take it when I come back.)

= They will come again one way or another. (So don't even bother asking them to come back.)

Track
13

2. 제가 할 수 있는 일이 아니에요.

= It is not something that I can do.

→ 어차피 제가 할 수 있는 일이 아니에요.

= Even if I try, it is not something that I can do.

= Don't bother asking me. It is not something that I can do.

= It is already obvious. I cannot do it.

3. 늦었으니까 빨리 와.

= You are late, so hurry up!

→ 어차피 늦었으니까 천천히 와.

= You are late anyway, so take your time.

= Even if you hurry now, you are already very late, so just take your time.

Sample Sentences

어차피 못 해요.

= It is obvious I cannot do it.

어차피 늦었으니까 오지 마.

= You are already late, so don't come. (You can say this to a friend who is running late.)

어차피 해야 되는 거니까, 재미있게 해요.

= One way or another, you have to do it anyway, so (you would better) try to have fun while doing it.

어차피 저도 지금 거기 가는 중이에요.

= I am on my way there anyway.

= Even if you had not asked me, I am already in the middle of going there anyway, so don't worry.

Track 13

Sample Dialogue

Track
14

현우: 석진 씨, 가방 안 가져가요?

석진: 아, 어차피 이따가 사무실에 다시
　　올 거예요.

현우: 아, 퇴근하기 전에 사무실 들를
　　거예요?

석진: 네.

*Hyunwoo: Seokjin, you're not going to take your
bag?*

*Seokjin: Oh, I'm going to come back to the office
in a little bit anyway.*

*Hyunwoo: Oh, so you'll come back to the office
before leaving work?*

Seokjin: Yes.

51

Exercises for Lesson 7

Translate the following English sentences into Korean sentences using 어차피.

1. I will come back anyway.

→

2. You are late anyway, so take your time.

→

3. Even if I try, it is not something that I can do.

→

4. One way or another, you have to do it anyway, so (you would better) try to have fun while doing it.

→

Check the answers on **p.209**

52

LESSON 8

I am not sure if ...

-(으)ㄴ/는지 잘 모르겠어요

Track 15

In this lesson, let's take a look at how to say "I am not sure if..." in Korean. First of all, you need to remember that this is not going to be translated word for word.

"To be sure" and "to not be sure" in Korean

The word for "to be sure" or "to be certain" in Korean is 확실하다. Therefore, the literal translation of "to not be sure" is 확실하지 않다, but this form is not commonly used in everyday spoken Korean.

확 = certain

실 is used in the word 사실 which means "a fact".

"Are you sure?"

When asking someone if they are sure or certain of something, you can still use the word 확실하다 and say, "확실해요?". Sometimes you can also say, "정말이에요?" if you want to say,

53

"Are you serious?" or "Is that real?".

How to say "I am not sure"

The most natural Korean expression for "I am not sure" is, "잘 모르겠어요." The word 모르다 means "to not know" and if you say, "잘 몰라요" it means, "I do not know well" or "I do not know much (about it)."

> **Ex)**
> 스포츠 잘 몰라요. = I do not know about sports.

Track 15

The suffix -겠- adds the nuance of assumption or intention (-겠- will be covered in more detail in a future lesson in Level 6), so when you say, "모르겠어요", you mean, "I do not seem to know" or "I would like to know, but I really do not."

"잘 모르겠어요" means the same thing as "모르겠어요" because you do not actually need to use the word 잘, but "잘 모르겠어요" is such a common and fixed expression that many Korean people use it to mean "I am not sure." or "I do not know for sure."

How to say "I am not sure if…"

"If ___ or not" or "whether or not" in Korean is expressed through the structure -(으)ㄴ/는지 (go back to Level 5 Lesson 18 to review).

-(으)ㄴ/는지 잘 모르겠어요 = I am not sure if…

You can use interrogative words (when/what/where/how/who/why/which) with this structure, too.

Present Tense

-(으)ㄴ/는지 잘 모르겠어요.

Ex)

이거 누구 책인지 잘 모르겠어요.

= I am not sure whose book this is.

Past Tense

-았/었/였는지 잘 모르겠어요.

Ex)

다 끝났는지 잘 모르겠어요.

= I am not sure if it all ended.

Track
15

Future Tense

-(으)ㄹ지 잘 모르겠어요.

-(으)ㄹ 건지 잘 모르겠어요.

Ex)

서점이 내일 문을 열지 잘 모르겠어요.

= I am not sure if the bookstore will be open tomorrow.

서점이 내일 문을 열 건지 잘 모르겠어요.

= I am not sure if the bookstore will be open tomorrow.

If you want to add "or not" at the end, you can use the structure Verb stem + -(으)ㄴ/는지 + Verb stem + 안 -(으)ㄴ/는지.

Sample Sentences

어디로 갈지 잘 모르겠어요.

= I am not sure where we will go.

내일 만날지 안 만날지 잘 모르겠어요.

= I am not sure if we will meet tomorrow or not.

    * If you want to emphasize "we" you can add 우리 at the beginning of the sentence.

여기가 맞는지 잘 모르겠어요.

= I am not sure if this is the right place.

뭘 해야 될지 잘 모르겠어요.

= I am not sure what to do.

= I am not sure what I (will) have to do.

Track 15

이게 무슨 뜻인지 잘 모르겠어요.

= I am not sure what this means.

    * 이게 has the same meaning as 이것이 which means "this is".

56

Sample Dialogue

경은: 경화 씨, 요즘도 요가 열심히 다녀요?

경화: 네.

경은: 어때요? 요가 하니까 좋아요?

경화: 솔직히 좋은지 잘 모르겠어요.

Kyeong-eun: Kyung-hwa, are you still doing yoga?

Kyung-hwa: Yes.

Kyeong-eun: How is it? Is it good?

Kyung-hwa: Honestly, I'm not sure if it's good.

✎ Exercises for Lesson **8**

Translate the following English sentences into Korean sentences using -(으)ㄴ/는지 잘 모르겠어요.

1. I am not sure whose book this is.

....

2. I am not sure if the bookstore will open tomorrow.

....

3. I am not sure if it all ended.

....

4. I am not sure what this means.

....

5. I am not sure if we will meet tomorrow or not.

....

Check the answers on **p.209**

LESSON 9

While you are at it …

-(으)ㄴ/는 김에

Track
17

In this lesson, let's take a look at the expression -(으)ㄴ/는 김에 and how to use it to say things like "while you are there", "while I am at it", or "since you are going to do it".

The word 김 here is a noun that literally means "an opportunity" or "a reason to do something". It is NOT, however, commonly used on its own to mean "opportunity" or "reason". It is almost always used in the structure, -(으)ㄴ/는 김에.

-(으)ㄴ/는 김에

= While you are there

= While you are at it

= While I am there

= Since you are already going to do it

Usages

I. You can use -(으)ㄴ/는 김에 when talking about something (usually not originally planned)

59

that you do while you are doing something else because it is convenient, effective, or easy that way.

ex) While I was visiting the library, I also stopped by the post office inside it.

2. You can use -(으)ㄴ/는 김에 when you want to ask someone to do something for you while they are going somewhere or while they are already planning to do something.

ex) While you are at it, can you please make one for me, too?

3. You can use -(으)ㄴ/는 김에 when you want to suggest doing something based on the fact that you are already going to do something similar or near to the place where you already are.

> *Conjugation*
>
> You use -(으)ㄴ 김에 in past tense sentences and -는 김에 in present and future tense sentences.

Examples

1. 백화점에 가는 김에

= While I am/you are going to the department store...

   * The act of going (= 가다) has not happened yet, so it is in the present tense, 가는.

+ 영화도 볼 거예요. = I am also going to see a movie.

   → 백화점에 가는 김에 영화도 볼 거예요.

+ 서점에도 갈까요? = shall we go to the bookstore, too?

   → 백화점에 가는 김에 서점에도 갈까요?

2. 서울에 온 김에

= While you are/I am visiting Seoul... / Since you/I came to Seoul...

   * The act of coming (= 오다) has already happened, so it is in the past tense, 온.

+ 친구들을 만났어요. = I met some friends.

   → 서울에 온 김에 친구들을 만났어요.

+ 며칠 더 있을 거예요. = I am going to stay for a few more days.

   → 서울에 온 김에 며칠 더 있을 거예요.

Sample Sentences

도서관에 가는 김에, 제 책도 반납해 주세요.

= While you are going to the library (Since you are going to the library anyway), please return my book, too.

Track 17

도서관에 간 김에 제 책도 빌려 주세요.

= While you are at the library, check out some books for me, too.

여기 온 김에 커피 마실까요?

= While we are here, shall we have some coffee?

   * You can also say "여기 왔으니까 커피 마실까요?" since it has a similar meaning, but using 김에 can mean you were originally there to do something else.

시작한 김에 제가 끝까지 할게요.

= While I am doing it (Since I have started it anyway), I will finish it (I will do it until it is finished).

61

밖에 나간 김에 제 부탁 하나만 들어주세요.

= While you are outside, please do me a favor.

말이 나온 김에, 우리 피자 먹을까요?

= Speaking of which, shall we have some pizza?

    * 말이 나온 김에 is a fixed phrase and means "speaking of which/now that we are

    talking about it".

Track 17

Sample Dialogue

석진: 태호야, 뭐 해?

태호: 응, 라면 끓여.

석진: 그래? 그럼 끓이는 김에 내 것도 부탁해.

Seokjin: Taeho, what are you doing?

Taeho: I'm making ramyeon.

Seokjin: Oh yeah? While you're at it, make me some too.

by Expressing Doubts, Abilities, and Happenings

✏️ Exercises for Lesson **9**

Fill in the blanks using -(으)ㄴ/는 김에.

1. (   ) 제 책도 반납해 주세요.

   = While you are going to the library (Since you are going to the library anyway), please return my book, too.

2. (   ) 우리 피자 먹을까요?

   = Speaking of which, shall we have some pizza?

3. (   ) 며칠 더 있을 거예요.

   = While I am visiting Seoul (Since I came to Seoul), I am going to stay for a few extra days.

4. (   ) 제가 끝까지 할게요.

   = While I am doing it (Since I have started it anyway), I will finish it (I will do it until it is finished).

Check the answers on **p.209**

LESSON **10**

Sentence Building Drill 6

Sentence Building Drill 6

Track
19

In this series, we focus on how you can use the grammatical rules and expressions that you have learned so far to train yourself to comfortably and flexibly make more Korean sentences.

We will start off with THREE key sentences, then practice changing parts of these sentences so that you do not end up just memorizing the same three sentences. We want you to be able to be as flexible as possible with the Korean sentences that you can make.

Key Sentence (1)

우리 어차피 늦을 것 같은데, 다음에 갈까요?

= It looks like we are going to be late anyway. Shall we go next time?

Key Sentence (2)

일하는 중이어서 전화 못 받으니까 나중에 전화할게요.

= I am in the middle of working so I cannot take the call, so I will call you later.

Key Sentence (3)

여기가 제가 제일 자주 가는 카페들 중 한 곳인데, 같이 가 볼래요?

= This is one of the cafés that I visit most often. Do you want to go there together?

Expansion & Variation Practice with Key Sentence (1)

0. Original Sentence:

우리 어차피 늦을 것 같은데, 다음에 갈까요?

= It looks like we are going to be late anyway. Shall we go next time?

* If you want to say "either way/in one way or another", you can add 어차피.

** -(으)ㄹ까요? is how to say, "Shall we do [something]?" in Korean.

1.

우리 어차피 늦을 거예요. = We are going to be late anyway.

어차피 *늦었어요. = Whatever we do, we are already late.

어차피 이거 지금 못 해요. = One way or another, I cannot do this now.

* In Korean, when you say you are late, you must use the past tense since you are already in the state of being late.

2.

다음에 갈까요? = Shall we go next time?

내일 할까요? = Shall we do it tomorrow?

같이 할까요? = Shall we do it together?

Expansion & Variation Practice with Key Sentence (2)

0. Original Sentence:

일하는 중이어서 전화 못 받으니까 나중에 전화할게요.

= I am in the middle of working so I cannot take the call, so I will call you later.

* -(으)니까 means "since/therefore".

1.

일하는 중이에요. = I am (in the middle of) working.

공부하는 중이에요. = I am (in the middle of) studying.

책 읽는 중이었어요. = I was (in the middle of) reading a book.

뭐 하는 중이었어요? = What were you doing?

Track 19

2.

지금 전화 못 받으니까 나중에 전화할게요.

= I cannot answer the phone now so I will call you later.

오늘 바쁘니까 내일 만나요.

= I am busy today so let's meet tomorrow.

밖에 비 오니까 우산 가져가세요.

= It is raining outside so take your umbrella with you.

이거 무거우니까 같이 들어요.

= It is heavy so let's lift it together.

이거 무거우니까 *현우 씨가 들어요.

= It is heavy so you lift it, Hyunwoo.

* When you want to say, "You lift it", you should say the person's name or job title rather than 당신.

67

Expansion & Variation Practice with Key Sentence (3)

0. Original Sentence:

여기가 제가 제일 자주 가는 카페들 중 한 곳인데, 같이 가 볼래요?

= This is one of the cafés that I visit most often. Do you want to go there together?

* This sentence can be broken down into two main parts. The first part is how to say one of the things or places that you do/have/go.

Ex)

제가 제일 자주 가는 카페들 중 한 **곳이에요.

= It is one of the cafés that I visit most often.

** You can use the word 곳 as a counter since it is a place. If you want to say a person, you can say 한 명.

Track 19

I.

제가 제일 자주 가는 카페들 중 한 곳이에요.

= It is one of the cafés that I visit most often.

제가 제일 자주 만나는 친구들 중 한 명이에요.

= He/She is one of my friends that I meet most often.

제가 제일 좋아하는 영화들 중 *하나예요.

= It is one of the movies that I like the most.

* In this case you would use 하나 as it is the most commonly used.

2.

같이 가 볼래요?

= Do you want to go (check out the place) together?

내일 만날래요?

= Do you want to meet tomorrow?

*친구들 만날 건데, 같이 갈래요?

= I am going to meet my friends. Do you want to go there together?

이거 마셔 볼래요?

= Do you want to try drinking this?

* If you want to say these phrases separately, you can say, "친구들 만날 거예요. 같이 갈래요?"

Track
19

by Expressing Doubts, Abilities, and Happenings

Sample Dialogue

🎙
Track
20

캐시: 제가 제일 좋아하는 한국 과자예요. 먹어 볼래요?

석진: 지금 게임 하는 중이니까 이따가 먹어 볼게요.

캐시: 무슨 게임 해요?

Cassie: This is my favorite Korean snack. Do you want to try it?

Seokjin: I'm in the middle of a game, so I'll try it later.

Cassie: What game are you playing?

✏ Exercises for Lesson 10

Translate each phrase or sentence into Korean and write it on the lines provided.

1. I am (in the middle of) working.

....

2. We are going to be late anyway.

....

3. I am busy today so let's meet tomorrow.

....

4. Shall we go next time?

....

5. He/She is one of my friends that I meet most often.

....

Check the answers on **p.209**

71

by Expressing Doubts, Abilities, and Happenings

BLOG

Yongdu-am and Yongyeon on Jeju Island
(제주도 용두암과 용연)

Anyone that has been to Jeju Island, Korea's largest island, will tell you how wonderful it is. Some will go on about the beauty of its oceans and coastlines, some will share their experience hiking up Halla Mountain, while others will talk about Jeju's overall charm and serenity.

But how many of you have heard Jeju Island's folk stories and legends? I currently live on Jeju Island in Jeju City to be exact. You don't have to go too far to see one of Jeju's famous rocks and hear its story. The rock I am talking about is 용두암 (Yongdu-am or Dragon Head Rock). Because Jeju was formed by a volcano, you can see many basalt rock formations; Dragon Head Rock is one of those formations... or is it?

The rock itself is 10 meters tall and 30 meters long and juts out of the ocean on the coastline in Jeju City. The legend says that a dragon tried to steal a jade stone which made the Halla Mountain god furious. As the dragon was flying off with his newly stolen prize, the god reached for his bow and arrow and shot at the dragon. The arrow struck the dragon causing him to fall into the ocean. His body began to sink and while he was looking up at the sky above the water, his head froze. It almost seems like poetic justice, since the sky was the dragon's favorite place but is now forced to forever look up knowing he will never be able to fly again.

Dragon Head Rock brings in thousands of visitors every year hoping to catch a glimpse. In Korea, people believe that black dragons are symbols of bravery, hope, and good luck. So, if you are ever in Jeju City, take some time to check out this incredible site.

* Tip: If you do plan on visiting Dragon Head Rock, I highly suggest checking it out at night. There is a light that shines on its head which creates a stunning sight.

If you travel just a bit farther east from Dragon Head Rock, you can see the place where the dragon of Dragon Head Rock used to play, according to the legend. 용연 (Yong-yeon or Dragon Pond) was formed by fresh water running down a mountain valley. There is a wooden bridge that crosses the pond and gives visitors a wonderful view. One of the legends here is that the pond was actually created by the water running off the back of a dragon after ascending to heaven. That is how the pond got its name: Yong-yeon, or Dragon Pond.

This is just one of many legends from Jeju Island. Another one I'd like to share revolves around Jeju's goddess, Seolmundae Halmang. She was a very large and strong goddess and would carry dirt in her skirt. As she walked around in the ocean, some of the dirt would fall through holes in her skirt, which began to form the island now known as Jeju. It seemed she was pleased with how the volcanic cones were forming so decided to make some of them taller. If she felt some of them were too tall, she would rip off the top part; this gave them their caved-in peaks. She made Halla Mountain the tallest mountain and placed it in the center of the island. However, she thought it was too tall as well so took off the top portion and threw it in the ocean. This part is now Sanbangsan, which is located in Seogwipo. If you look at the top of Sanbangsan, it looks like a dome and seems like it would fit perfectly in the caved-in cone on Halla Mountain's peak.

This is how Jeju Island and its mountains are thought to be made. If you dig into the history of Jeju, you will find many myths and legends about how things were created or started. I highly recommend looking up some of the legends the next time you are in Jeju. They will make your experience that much more fun.

Written by Johnny Bland

LESSON **11**

I mean …

> # 그러니까, 제 말은, -(이)라고요, 말이에요

Track 21

In this lesson, let's take a look at how to say "I mean..." in Korean. There are many ways of saying this expression in Korean, and it has various usages in English, too. Here, we would like to introduce four main ways to express "I mean..." in Korean.

How to Say "to mean" in Korean

Most English-Korean dictionaries will introduce the word 의미하다 as the first translation of the verb "to mean", but in Korean 의미하다 sounds very formal, so therefore it is not used in everyday conversation. When you want to say, **"ABC means XYZ",** you can say, **"ABC + -은/는 + XYZ + -라는 뜻이에요".**

> **Ex)**
> ABC + -은/는 + XYZ + -라는 뜻이에요.

The word 뜻 is a noun defined as "meaning", and when used with the verb -이다, it becomes 뜻이다, or, "It is the meaning". When used with -라는, which works as a quoting marker, -라는

76

뜻이다 means "It is the meaning of..." or "It has the meaning of...".

In spoken language, you will hear 뜻 more than 의미. 의미 is more formal and is used more often in written language.

How to Say "I mean/you mean..." in Korean

I. 그러니까

When you want to reassure someone of what you are saying or to make your point one more time, you can use 그러니까. In this context, 그러니까 can be translated as "so..." in English. After you say 그러니까, you summarize what you said before or make a more detailed explanation. Depending on the context, however, in Korean, this can be used to mean "You mean..." when you are checking with the other person on what he or she has said.

Track 21

2. 제 말 뜻은 or 제 말은

When you want to make sure that the other person can understand what you are saying, and you want to rephrase something you have already said, you can say, "제 말 뜻은 (= What I mean is...)" or "제 말은 (= What I am saying is...)". If you want to say "You mean..." you should say the person's name.

> **Ex)** 현우 씨 말은...

3. -(이)라고요 or -(ㄴ/은/는)다고요

When you start a sentence with 그러니까 or 제 말 뜻은, you normally end the sentence with -라고요 or -다고요. -라고 and -다고 are both verb endings that are used to quote or cite what someone has said. Since you are delivering your point one more time with "I mean...", you need to use the endings -라고 or -다고. The word -요 at the end is, as you know, used to make your sentence polite. -(이)라고요 is used after nouns and -다고요 is used after verb stems. If your sentence after "I mean..." is an imperative sentence, you should use -(으)라고요.

4. (-(이)라는/-다는) 말이에요

In addition to -라고요 and -다고요, another commonly used sentence ending for saying
"I mean..." in Korean is (-(이)라는/-다는) 말이에요. Here, the word 말 means "words" or
"phrases", and -라는 or -다는 is used to quote or cite what someone has said. -라는 is used
after nouns, and -다는 is used after verb stems.

Sample Sentences

홍대, 그러니까 홍익대학교에 가 보셨어요?

= Have you been to Hongdae, I mean, Hongik University?

Track 21

그러니까 이거 저 준다고요?

= You mean you are giving this to me?

= I mean, you are giving this to me?

= So (I mean/you mean) you are giving this to me?

그러니까, 벌써 다 했다고요.

= I mean, I already finished it.

    * If you say "벌써 다 했어요", you are missing the nuance that you are upset or annoyed.

그러니까 제 말은, 이 일에는 이 사람이 최고라고요.

= I mean, for this work, this person is the best.

그러니까 혼자 간다는 말이에요?

= You mean you are going there alone?

= I mean, you are going there alone?

Using "I mean..." to Correct What You have Said

When you want to say "I mean" in the middle of a sentence to correct yourself, you can say 아니 in Korean.

Ex)

I went there last Saturday, I mean, Sunday.

= 지난주 토요일에, 아니, 일요일에 갔어요.

Give me this one, I mean, this one.

= 이거, 아니, 이거 주세요.

How to Say "I mean it" in Korean

Track 21

When "I mean it" is used as a fixed expression, the most commonly used equivalent in Korean is, "**진짜예요.**" or "**진심이에요.**"

Sample Dialogue

🎤 Track 22

캐시: 이 운동화 어때요?

제시카: 오! 제가 좋아하는 스타일이에요.
근데 색깔이 엄청 화려하네요.

캐시: 그러니까 좋다는 말이에요, 싫다는
말이에요?

제시카: 다른 색깔은 없어요?

Cassie: How are these sneakers?

*Jessica: Oh! I like that style. But the color is really
bright.*

*Cassie: So do you mean you like them or dislike
them?*

Jessica: Isn't there a different color?

✎ Exercises for Lesson 11

Fill in the boxes provided to match the English translation.

1. 그러니까 이거 저 ⬜⬜⬜⬜ ?

   = You mean you are giving this to me?

2. 그러니까 혼자 ⬜⬜⬜ ⬜⬜⬜⬜ ?

   = You mean you are going there alone?

3. 지난주 토요일에, ⬜⬜ , 일요일에 갔어요.

   = I went there last Saturday, I mean, Sunday.

4. 그러니까 ⬜ ⬜⬜ , 이 일에는 이 사람이 최고라고요.

   = I mean, for this work, this person is the best.

Check the answers on **p.209**

81

LESSON **12**

What do you mean? What does that mean?

무슨 말이에요?

In the previous lesson, we introduced the phrase "I mean…" and some various ways to use it in Korean. In this lesson, let's take a look at how to ask someone in Korean, "What do you mean?", "What does that mean?", or "What is that supposed to mean?" when you cannot believe what you have just heard or when you do not understand someone's remark or point very well.

무슨 말이에요?

= What do you mean?

= What is that supposed to mean?

= What does that mean?

= What are you talking about?

무엇 and 뭐 mean the same thing, and if you want to make it into an adjective, you would say 무슨.

무슨 means "what kind of" or "which" and 말 means "word" or "language". Therefore, 무슨 말 means "what word", "which word", or "what kind of things (to be said or written)".

"무슨 말이에요?" literally means, "What word/language is it?", but it is more correctly translated as, "What do you mean?" You can use "무슨 말이에요?" when you are in disbelief after you hear someone say something or when you have not clearly understood what they mean.

Between friends, you can say, "무슨 말이야?"

> **Ex)**
> A: 카메라 팔 거예요.
>   (I am going to sell my camera.)
> B: 무슨 말이에요? 카메라도 없잖아요.
>   (What do you mean? You do not even have a camera!)

🎙️
Track 23

무슨 소리예요?

"무슨 소리예요?" is the same as "무슨 말이에요?" but it is less formal and less polite. Therefore, it is not advised to use it with someone older than you or someone to whom you are supposed to be polite. This is because 말 means "words", but 소리 means "sounds". You do not want to refer to the words of the other person as mere "sounds". You can use 무슨 소리예요? more safely, however, when you are literally saying, "What is that sound?"

무슨 말씀이세요?

In Korean, there are many ways of making a phrase "honorific", and one of the ways is to use "honorific" nouns. 말씀 is the honorific version of 말.

How to Literally Ask, "What does this mean?"

As we have introduced in the previous lesson, when you want to LITERALLY ask what a certain expression means, you can use the expression, "무슨 뜻이에요?"

Sample Sentences

네? 그게 무슨 말이에요?

= What? What do you mean?

= Huh? What does THAT mean?

Track 23

그만둘 거라고요? 갑자기 무슨 말이에요?

= You are going to quit? What do you mean all of a sudden?

무슨 말이에요? 제가 왜요?

= What do you mean? Why (do) I (have to...)?

= What do you mean? Why me?

무슨 말인지 잘 모르겠어요.

= I am not sure what you mean.

= I do not know what you are talking about.

무슨 말인지 알겠어요.

= I know what you mean.

= I understand what you are saying.

Sample Dialogue

Track 24

경화: 석진 씨, 주연 씨 생일 선물 저랑 같이
할래요?

석진: 네? 무슨 말이에요? 주연 씨 생일
지난달이었잖아요.

경화: 아! 주연 씨 말고 경은 씨요.

*Kyung-hwa: Seokjin, shall we buy Jooyeon's
birthday present together?*

*Seokjin: Huh? What do you mean? Jooyeon's
birthday was last month.*

Kyung-hwa: Ah! Not Jooyeon, Kyeong-eun.

✎ Exercises for Lesson 12

Answer the following questions.

1. What does "무슨 말이에요?" mean in English?

....

2. What is the less formal and less polite version of "무슨 말이에요?"

....

3. What is the honorific version of 말?

....

4. By using the honorific version of 말, write "무슨 말이에요?" in honorific form.

....

5. How do you say when you want to literally ask what a certain expression means?

....

Check the answers on **p.209**

LESSON **13**

Word Builder 10

과(過)

Word Builder lessons are designed to help you understand how to expand your vocabulary by learning and understanding some common and basic building blocks of Korean words. The words and letters introduced through Word Builder lessons are not necessarily all Chinese characters, or 한자. Though many of them are based on Chinese characters, the meanings can be different from modern-day Chinese. Your goal through these lessons is to understand how words are formed and then remember the keywords in Korean to expand your Korean vocabulary from there. You certainly do not have to memorize the Hanja characters, but if you want to, feel free!

Track
25

In this lesson, we are looking at the key word element 과. When 과 is written in Hanja as 過, it means "to surpass", "to go over", "to pass", or "too much".

과 (to surpass, too much) + 식 (eat) = 과식 過食 = eating too much, overeating

과 (to surpass, too much) + 속 (to be fast) = 과속 過速 = speeding

통 (to go through) + 과 (to pass) = 통과 通過 = pass, passing through, passing (a test)

* Passing a big exam such as a college entrance exam is called 합격, which means "pass". When it is a simple quiz or physical test, you will hear 통과.

Ex)

터널을 통과하다

= to pass through a tunnel

간 (to see) + 과 (to pass) = 간과 看過 = failure to notice, passing over

과 (too much) + 민 (agile, quick) = 과민 過敏 = being hypersensitive

Track 25

Related Vocabulary

과민 반응 過敏 反應 = overreaction

Ex)

과민 반응 하지 마.

= Don't overreact.

과 (too much) + 로 (labor) = 과로 過勞 = working too much, too much labor

Ex)

과로하지 마세요.

= Don't work too hard.

과 (to pass) + 거 (to go) = 과거 過去 = the past

Related Vocabulary

과거 시제 過去 時制 ＝ the past tense

과 (to surpass, too much) ＋ 대 (to be big) ＝ 과대 過大 ＝ too big, oversized
* This is used with other words, not on its own.

Related Vocabulary

과대 포장 過大 包裝 ＝ oversized package
과대평가 過大評價 ＝ overestimate

과 (to pass) ＋ 정 (way, limit) ＝ 과정 過程 ＝ process

과 (to surpass, too much) ＋ 소비 (consumption) ＝ 과소비 過消費 ＝ overspending, excessive consumption

Track 25

Related Vocabulary

소비자 消費者 ＝ consumer

과 (too much) ＋ 신 (to believe) ＝ 과신 過信 ＝ overconfidence

Sample Dialogue

Track
26

캐시: 와, 이것 좀 보세요.

경화: 왜요?

캐시: 봉투가 이렇게 큰데, 과자가 이만큼밖에 안 들어 있어요.

경화: 요즘 과대 포장 너무 심한 것 같아요.

Cassie: Whoa, look at this.

Kyung-hwa: What is it?

Cassie: The bag is so big, but there's only this much inside.

Kyung-hwa: I think excessive packaging is ridiculous these days.

✎ Exercises for Lesson *13*

Fill in the blanks with the appropriate Sino-Korean word from the lesson.

1. The key word element (   ) is related to "to surpass", "to go over", "to pass", or "too much".

2. (   ) = eating too much, overeating

3. (   ) = speeding

4. (   ) = working too much, too much labor

5. (   ) = process

Check the answers on **p.209**

LESSON 14

So one can also + verb

동사 + -(으)ㄹ 겸

Track 27

In this lesson, let's take a look at the expression -(으)ㄹ 겸 and how it is used. -(으)ㄹ 겸 is used to express something or an action that has dual purposes or positions. It can be translated as "/ [slash]" or "and" when used with nouns, and as "(while doing something else) to do XYZ as well" when used with verbs.

겸

When you want to say "breakfast/lunch" or "singer/actor", you use the word **겸**.

Ex)

아침 겸 점심 = breakfast/lunch, brunch

가수 겸 배우 = singer and actor, singer/actor

화가 겸 작곡가 = painter/composer, painter and composer

-(으)ㄹ 겸

When you want to talk about an action that has two or more purposes, you can list them using -(으)ㄹ 겸. When you just mention one purpose using -(으)ㄹ 겸 in a sentence, the other purpose has to be understood from the context. Since -(으)ㄹ 겸 usually has the nuance of "both at the same time", you often use the particle -도 (meaning "also") after the noun that comes before "Verb + -(으)ㄹ 겸".

Sample Sentences

바람 좀 쐴 겸 밖에 나왔어요.

= (There is another reason/purpose, too, but) I came outside to get some fresh air.

> * 바람 좀 쐬다 = To get some breeze/fresh air.

Track 27

영어 공부도 할 겸, 영어로 된 소설을 읽고 있어요.

= (I am doing it because it is fun, too, but) I am reading a novel written in English to study English as well.

> * You are using -(으)ㄹ 겸 when there are additional or hidden reasons for doing something. However, you would not use it when there is only one purpose. There should be at least two purposes.

친구 생일 선물도 살 겸, 제 옷도 볼 겸, 백화점에 갈 거예요.

= I am going to go to the department store to buy a present for my friend's birthday, and at the same time, look for some clothes for myself.

> * If you are only going to buy your friend's birthday present, you would just say, "친구 생일 선물 사러 갈 거예요."

산책도 할 겸, 사진도 찍을 겸, 남산에 갔어요.

= I went to Nam Mountain to take a walk and also to take some photos.

-(으)ㄹ 겸 해서

Sometimes, when people feel that just saying -(으)ㄹ 겸 is a little too short, they add the word 해서 after it and say, -(으)ㄹ 겸 해서. It has the same meaning as -(으)ㄹ 겸, but -(으)ㄹ 겸 해서 is usually used with the second verb when there are two verbs used as "purposes" for doing something.

If the other person already knows what you are doing, you do not have to repeat that part. You can just end the sentence with -(으)ㄹ 겸 해서(요).

Ex)
산책도 할 겸, 사진도 찍을 겸 = 산책도 할 겸, 사진도 찍을 겸 해서.

Track 27

Sample Dialogue

딸: 엄마, 뭐 살 거 있어요? 저 운전 연습도 할 겸 마트 갔다 올게요.

엄마: 그래? 그럼 계란이랑 식빵 좀 사 와. 나가는 김에 쓰레기도 버려 주면 더 좋고.

딸: 네. 갔다 올게요.

Daughter: Mom, do you need anything? I want to practice driving so I'm going to the store.

Mom: Really? Then buy some eggs and bread. I'd appreciate it if you also took out the trash while you're at it.

Daughter: Okay. I'll be back soon.

95

✏ Exercises for Lesson 14

Check the answers on **p.209**

Complete the sentences by conjugating the word(s) in the parentheses with -(으)ㄹ 겸.

1. 바람 좀 .... 밖에 나왔어요. (쐬다)

= (There is another reason/purpose, too, but) I came outside to get some fresh air.

2. 영어 공부도 ...., 영어로 된 소설을 읽고 있어요. (하다)

= (I am doing it because it is fun, too, but) I am reading a novel written in English to study English as well.

3. 산책도 ...., 사진도 ...., 남산에 갔어요. (하다, 찍다)

= I went to Nam Mountain to take a walk and also to take some photos.

4. 친구 생일 선물도 ...., 제 옷도 ...., 백화점에 갈 거예요. (사다, 보다)

= I am going to go to the department store to buy a present for my friend's birthday, and at the same time, look for some clothes for myself.

LESSON 15

The thing that is called …, What they call …

-(이)라는 것은

Track
29

In Korean, when you are talking about the definition of something or when you want to express what you think is the definition or the nature of something, you can use the expression -(이)라는 것은. It can be followed by various types of sentence endings, including -라고 생각해요 (I think that...), -인 것 같아요 (It seems that...), etc.

-(이)라는 것은

-(이)라는 것은 is a shortened form of -(이)라고 하는 것은. The structure -(이)라고 하다 means "to say...", and 것 means "thing" or "fact", so together, -(이)라고 하는 것 means "the thing that is called..." or "what they call...".

You use this expression when you are trying to define something or when giving advice to younger people. It can also be used to share your own opinion.

Examples

부자라는 것은

= What they call 부자 is...

= A rich man is...

= (I think that) A rich man is...

자유라는 것은

= What they call 자유 is...

= Freedom is...

= (I think that) Freedom is...

우정이라는 것은

= What they call "friendship" is...

= Friendship is...

Track 29

사람의 마음이라는 것은

= I think a person's mind/heart is...

More Examples

사랑이라는 것은 = Love is...

삶이라는 것은 = Life is...

꿈이라는 것은 = A dream is...

* These expressions are typically used when someone is teaching or preaching.

Shortening -(이)라는 것은 to -(이)란

To make it easier to say, people often shorten -(이)라는 것은 to -(이)란.

Ex)

사랑이라는 것은 → 사랑이란

삶이라는 것은 → 삶이란

꿈이라는 것은 → 꿈이란

자유라는 것은 → 자유란

우정이라는 것은 → 우정이란

사람의 마음이라는 것은 → 사람의 마음이란

Track 29

Sample Sentences

사랑이란 무엇일까요?

= What is love?

사랑이란 쉽지 않아요.

= Love is not easy.

자유라는 것은, 아무거나 마음대로 하는 것이 아니에요.

= Freedom does not mean doing whatever (you want to do) in any way you like.

진정한 친구란 어려울 때 도와주는 친구예요.

= A true friend is a friend who helps (you) when things are difficult.

Sample Dialogue

Track 30

수근: 지원 씨, 요즘 피츠버그 파이어리츠
　　　성적이 안 좋아서 어떡해요?

지원: 진정한 팬이란 팀 성적이 안 좋을 때도
　　　꾸준히 응원하는 팬이죠.

수근: 오! 멋있어요.

Soogeun: Jiwon, the Pittsburgh Pirates' scores aren't very good these days, so what are you going to do?

Jiwon: People who call themselves true fans are fans who cheer on their team even when their scores are bad.

Soogeun: Oh! You're admirable.

✎ Exercises for Lesson 15

Change the simple "A is..." phrases to "What they call A is..." phrases.

1. 부자는 → ( )

   = A rich man is...   = What they call 부자 is...

                                    = (I think that) A rich man is...

2. 자유는 → ( )

   = Freedom is...   = What they call 자유 is...

                                    = (I think that) Freedom is...

3. 우정은 → ( )

   = Friendship is...   = What they call "friendship" is...

                                    = (I think that) Friendship is...

4. 꿈은 → ( )

   = A dream is...   = What they call a "dream" is...

                                    = (I think that) A dream is...

Check the answers on **p.210**

LESSON 16

Various Usages of the Suffix -겠-

-겠-

Track 31

In this lesson, let's take a look at the suffix -겠-. It is commonly used in everyday Korean, but often not understood very well by learners, mainly because it has so many different meanings and usages.

Various Usages of **-겠-**

You can use -겠- to ask someone's intention, to express what you are going to do, to talk about something that will happen, to show your assumption about something, or to talk about possibilities or capabilities. It is also often used in fixed expressions such as "처음 뵙겠습니다 (= Nice to meet you)", "잘 먹겠습니다 (= Thank you for the food)", and *"다녀오겠습니다. (= I will see you later.)"

* 다녀오겠습니다 is typically said by kids to their parents when they leave the house.

Basically, -겠- is used to express one's intention or assumption.

1. -시겠어요? / -시겠습니까? = Would you...?, Would you like to...?

This phrase is only used in very formal Korean. In more casual Korean, you can use -(으)ㄹ래(요)? (review Level 4 Lesson 2 for this grammar point). The honorific suffix -시- is always used with -겠- in this case.

Ex)
어디로 가시겠어요?

= Where would you like to go?

2. -겠- (used to express one's intention) = I am going to..., I would like to...

Mostly used in formal Korean, -겠- can also express one's intention to do something. In more casual Korean, the same meaning can be expressed through -(으)ㄹ게(요) (review Level 3 Lesson 6 for this grammar point).

Track 31

Ex)
제가 하겠습니다.

= I will do it.

말하지 않겠습니다.

= I will not tell you.

= I will not speak to you.

3. -겠- (used to express one's opinion/idea/assumption) = I think..., I guess..., I assume...

This is the most common usage of -겠- for casual and everyday conversation in Korean. You can use -겠- to show your opinion or assumption about something or what will happen, but

103

you also give a nuance that you are somewhat careful with your opinion.

Ex)

아프겠어요.

= That must hurt.

    * If you are wanting to show an exclamation, you would say; "아프겠다!"

    ** You can also say, "아플 것 같아요" to mean, "That must hurt" or "I think it must

    be hurting a lot."

이게 좋겠어요.

= I think this will be good.

    * You can plainly say, "이게 좋아요 (= This is good)" to say the same thing, but if

    you would like to add your own assumption or opinion that this will be good for

    someone, you should say, "이게 좋겠어요."

Track 31

늦겠어요.

= (I think) I/we will be late.

    * If you are already late, you can say, "늦었어요" which means, "I am late."

When you want to express your assumption or ask someone else's opinion about a
possibility or a capability, you can use -겠-.

Ex)

혼자서도 되겠어요?

= Do you think you could handle it on your own?

이 상자 진짜 크네요. 저도 들어가겠어요.

= This box is so big. Even I would (be able to) fit in it.

* To a friend, you would say, "나도 들어가겠다. (= Even I would be able to fit in it.)"

4. -겠- used in fixed expressions

In addition to the usages above, -겠- is also commonly used in some fixed expressions.

Ex)

잘 먹겠습니다.

= (lit.) I will eat well.

= Thank you for the food.

    * This is sort of showing your intention but is more of a fixed expression.

알겠습니다.

= I got it. I understand.

Track 31

모르겠어요.

= I do not get it. I do not know. I am not sure.

힘들어 죽겠어요.

= I am so tired. This is so tough.

    * This expression is not saying you are really going to die. It is just expressing how hard something is.

졸려 죽겠어요.

= I am so tired, I am going to die.

Sample Dialogue

Track 32

효리: 요즘 야식을 너무 자주 먹었어요.
오늘부터 6시 이후에는 아무것도 안
먹겠어요.

윤아: 6시 이후에는 아무것도 안 먹겠다고요?
진짜 힘들겠다.

효리: 할 수 있어요.

*Hyori: I've eaten late-night snacks too often
recently. From today, I won't eat anything
after 6.*

*Yoona: You won't eat anything after 6? That
sounds hard.*

Hyori: I can do it.

🖊 Exercises for Lesson 16

Rewrite the sentences that end in **것 같아요** *using* **-겠**-.

1. 아플 것 같아요. = That must hurt.

　　→

2. 이게 좋을 것 같아요. = I think this will be good.

　　→

3. 이러다가 늦을 것 같아요. = At this rate, I think we will be late.

　　→

4. 힘들어 죽을 것 같아요. = I am so tired. This is so tough.

　　→

Check the answers on **P.210**

by Expressing Doubts, Abilities, and Happenings

LESSON **17**

Because, Since, Let me tell you...

-거든(요)

Track 33

In this lesson, let's take a look at the commonly used verb ending -거든(요). It has a very subtle meaning, and when used correctly and appropriately, it can make your Korean sound much more natural and fluent.

Usages of -거든(요)

1. -거든(요) can be used to express a reason or some background explanation for something, except -거든(요) forms a separate sentence from the sentence expressing a result. Other expressions that can express reasons for something are -아/어/여서, -(으)니까, and -기 때문에, but these are used in the same sentence with the result. However, -거든(요) is mostly added separately to your statement about what happened or will happen.

> **Ex)**
> 저도 모르겠어요. 저 방금 왔거든요.
> = I do not know either. I just got here.

You could say, "저 방금 왔어요" but by adding -거든요, you are adding flavor to your sentence and making it sound more natural. It is also showing a reason for your answer.

If you use -아/어/여서, -(으)니까, or -기 때문에 to say "because" or "since", the clause that explains the reason comes before your answer; with -거든요, the result usually comes first and the sentence that explains the reason comes next.

Ex)
저 방금 와서 저도 모르겠어요.
= I just got here so I do not know.

People sometimes say the -거든요 part of the sentence alone just to explain the reason for something, as long as the result is clear.

Track 33

Ex)
저 방금 왔거든요. = Because I just got here.

2. -거든(요) can also be used when you are implying that your story is continued. When you mention one thing in a sentence that ends with -거든(요), the other person will expect you to mention another thing that is related to what you just said in the next sentence.

Ex)
제가 지금 돈이 없거든요. 만 원만 빌려주세요.
= I do not have any money now. (So...) Please lend me just 10,000 won.

"**제가 지금 돈이 없어요. 만 원만 빌려 주세요**" has the same meaning, but by using -거든요, you are implying that you are not finished with your story.

Sample Sentences

제가 지금 좀 바쁘거든요.

= I am a little busy now, so...

아까 효진 씨 만났거든요. 그런데 이상한 말을 했어요.

= I met Hyojin earlier. But she said something strange.

> * If someone ends a sentence with -거든요, you do not want to interrupt them as they want to say more.

아직 말할 수 없어요. 비밀이거든요.

= I cannot tell you yet. (Because) It is a secret.

지난주에 제주도에 갔거든요. 그런데 계속 비가 왔어요.

= I went to Jeju Island last week. But it kept raining.

Track 33

내일은 안 바빠요. 오늘 일을 다 끝냈거든요.

= I am not busy tomorrow. (Because) I finished all the work today.

Generally, -거든요 is used when you want to soften your speech or express a reason for something indirectly, but sometimes when you are upset, you can use -거든요 as the sentence ending to express the reason that supports or explains your anger.

Sample Sentences

필요 없거든요!

= I do not need it!

이미 늦었거든요!

= It is already too late!

110

됐거든요!

= It is over. / I do not need that.

by Expressing Doubts, Abilities, and Happenings

Sample Dialogue

🎙
Track
34

경은: 오늘 지연 씨 표정이 안 좋네요.

경화: 지연 씨 몸살감기 걸렸거든요.

경은: 아, 진짜요? 지연 씨! 아프면 일찍
　　　퇴근해도 돼요.

Kyeong-eun: Jiyeon doesn't look too good today.

Kyung-hwa: It's because Jiyeon caught a bad cold.

*Kyeong-eun: Oh, really? Jiyeon, if you don't feel
well, you can leave work early.*

112

✏ Exercises for Lesson 17

Divide the phrases into two sentences using -거든요.

Ex)
저 방금 와서 저도 모르겠어요. → 저도 모르겠어요. 저 방금 왔거든요.

1. 오늘 일을 다 끝내서 내일은 안 바빠요.

→

2. 비밀이어서 아직 말할 수 없어요.

→

3. 제가 지금 좀 바빠서 이따가 전화할게요.

→

4. 제가 지금 돈이 없는데, 만 원만 빌려주세요.

→

Check the answers on **p.210**

113

LESSON **18**

Or

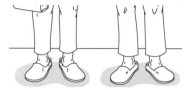

-(이)나, -거나, 아니면

Track 35

Welcome back to another Talk To Me In Korean lesson. Sometimes very simple words in English can become something more complicated in Korean and vice versa. Today's key expression is an example of that. In this lesson, let's learn how to say "or" in Korean.

The word "or" can be used to link nouns, adverbs, adjectives, verbs, or even sentences. You do not need multiple expression to say "or" in English, but in Korean, depending on what kind of word you are linking, the translations for "or" can be different.

Noun + OR + Noun

In order to link two nouns, you can use -(이)나.

After nouns that end with a consonant, add -이나.
After nouns that end with a vowel, add -나.

114

Ex)

공원이나 영화관 = a park or a movie theater

학생이나 선생님 = a student or a teacher

여기나 저기 = here or there

You can also use the word 아니면, which literally means "if not".

Ex)

공원 아니면 영화관

학생 아니면 선생님

여기 아니면 저기

Verb + OR + Verb

Track 35

Since adjectives are essentially "descriptive verbs" in Korean, adjectives and verbs are linked in the same manner. After verb stems, you can use -거나.

Ex)

먹거나 = eat or...

전화하거나 = make a phone call or...

집에 가거나 = go home or...

The tense (present, past, or future) is expressed through the last verb, so the last verb has to be conjugated accordingly to show the tense of the entire sentence.

Ex)

집에 가거나 친구를 만날 거예요. = I will (either) go home or meet a friend.

가다 is changed to 가거나 but you do not add -거나 to 만나다.

Sometimes people add -거나 to all of the phrases (Ex: 집에 가거나, 친구를 만나거나) and in that case, they use the verb 하다 (= to do) to finish the sentence.

Ex)
집에 가거나 친구를 만나거나 할 거예요.

In addition to using -거나 at the end of the sentence, you can add 아니면 as well between the two actions.

Ex)
집에 가거나 아니면 친구를 만날 거예요.

Track 35

* There are other ways of saying "or" with verbs, such as -든지 and -든가 but more on those in future lessons!

Sentence + OR + Sentence

In previous usages, we have seen that -(이)나 is used with nouns and -거나 is used with verbs. When you want to say "or" between two sentences, you simply use 아니면. 아니면 can be broken down into "아니다 (= to be not) + -(으)면 (= if)". 아니면 literally means "if not" or "if that is not the case".

Ex)
집에 갈 거예요? 아니면 친구를 만날 거예요?
= Are you going to go home? Or are you going to meet a friend?

이거 살 거예요? 아니면 다른 거 살 거예요?

= Are you going to buy this? Or are you going to buy something else?

You could say these sentences without 아니면, but it sounds more natural including it between the two sentences.

Sample Dialogue

Track 36

민종: 철우 씨, 철우 씨는 주말에 주로 뭐 해요?

철우: 집에서 밀린 청소 하거나 빨래해요.

민종: 밖에 잘 안 나가요?

철우: 가끔은 나가서 친구들도 만나죠. 아니면 자전거 타는 거 좋아해서 날씨 좋으면 자전거 타요.

Minjong: Cheol-woo, what do you usually do on the weekend?

Cheol-woo: I do cleaning that I've put off, or I do laundry.

Minjong: You don't go outside that often?

Cheol-woo: Sometimes I go out and meet friends. Or because I like to ride my bike, if the weather is nice I'll go for a bike ride.

✏ *Exercises for Lesson 18*

Fill in the blanks.

1. 공원 (   ) 영화관

   = a park or a movie theater

2. 학생 (   ) 선생님

   = a student or a teacher

3. 집에 (   ) 친구를 만날 거예요.

   = I will (either) go home or meet a friend.

4. 이거 살 거예요? (   ) 다른 거 살 거예요?

   = Are you going to buy this? Or are you going to buy something else?

Check the answers on **p.210**

LESSON 19

To improve, To change, To increase

-아/어/여지다 (Part 2)

Track 37

In Level 4 Lesson 28, we introduced the verb ending -아/어/여지다 and how it is used to express "to become + adjective".

Examples:

예쁘다 = to be pretty
예뻐지다 = to become pretty

조용하다 = to be silent
조용해지다 = to become silent

Some adjective words (or descriptive verbs) are so commonly used in the -아/어/여지다 form though that they are almost considered as independent verbs and have a single-word translation in English as well.

120

1. 달라지다

다르다 = to be different
다르 → 달라 + -아지다 = 달라지다 = to change, to become different

Sample Sentences

여기 많이 달라졌어요.

= This place has changed a lot.

뭔가 달라진 것 같아요.

= I feel like something has changed.

2. 좋아지다

좋다 = to be good, to be likeable
좋 → 좋 + -아지다 = 좋아지다 = to get better, to improve, to be enhanced, to start to like

Sample Sentences

이 가수가 좋아졌어요.

= I started to like this singer. = I like this singer now.

> * The verb literally means "to become better", but in this sentence, that does not really make sense. Therefore, you can say, "I like this singer now."

노래 실력이 좋아졌어요.

= My singing skills have improved.

> * It could mean going from bad to good, but in most cases, it tends to mean going from good to better.

Track 37

3. 많아지다

많다 = to be a lot, to be abundant
많 → 많 + -아지다 = 많아지다 = to increase

Sample Sentences

한국으로 여행 오는 사람들이 많아졌어요.
= The (number of) people who come to Korea for tourism have increased.
  * 증가하다 also means to increase, however, this word is not used as commonly as 많아지다.

학생이 많아졌어요.
= The (number of) students have increased.

Track 37

4. 없어지다

없다 = to be not there, to not exist, to not have
없 → 없 + -어지다 = 없어지다 = to disappear

Sample Sentences

제 핸드폰이 없어졌어요.
= My cellphone has disappeared.

아까 여기 있었는데 없어졌어요.
= It was here earlier but it disappeared.

Sample Dialogue

Track 38

현주: 우와! 사무실이 예전이랑 많이 달라졌네요?

경화: 네. 많이 좋아졌죠?

현주: 직원도 훨씬 많아졌네요?

경화: 네. 회사가 훨씬 커졌어요.

Hyunjoo: Wow! The office has changed a lot from before.

Kyung-hwa: Yeah. It's gotten a lot nicer, right?

Hyunjoo: There are more employees, too.

Kyung-hwa: Yes, the company has gotten much bigger.

123

✐ Exercises for Lesson 19

Fill in the blank for each sentence.

Check the answers on **p.210**

1. 여기 많이 (   ).

 = This place has changed a lot.

2. 뭔가 (   ) 것 같아요.

 = I feel like something has changed.

3. 제 핸드폰이 (   ).

 = My cellphone has disappeared.

4. 한국으로 여행 오는 사람들이 (   ).

 = The (number of) people who come to Korea for tourism have increased.

5. 노래 실력이 (   ).

 = My singing skills have improved.

LESSON **20**

Sentence Building Drill 7

Sentence Building Drill 7

Track
39

In this series, we focus on how you can use the grammatical rules and expressions that you have learned so far to train yourself to comfortably and flexibly make more Korean sentences.

We will start off with THREE key sentences, then practice changing parts of these sentences so that you do not end up just memorizing the same three sentences. We want you to be able to be as flexible as possible with the Korean sentences that you can make.

Key Sentence (1)
쇼핑도 할 겸, 친구도 만날 겸, 홍대에 갈 수도 있어요.
= I might go to Hongdae so I can do some shopping as well as meet a friend while I am there.

Key Sentence (2)
내일 다시 오거나, 아니면 다른 사람에게 부탁할게요.
= I will either come again tomorrow or ask someone else.

125

by Expressing Doubts, Abilities, and Happenings

Key Sentence (3)

그러니까, 누구하고 같이 갈 거라고요?

= So I mean, who did you say you were going to go with?

Expansion & Variation Practice with Key Sentence (1)

0. Original Sentence:

쇼핑도 할 겸, 친구도 만날 겸, 홍대에 갈 수도 있어요.

= I might go to Hongdae so I can do some shopping as well as meet a friend while I am there.

1.

친구도 만날 겸 = so I could meet a friend as well

공부도 할 겸 = to do some studying (as well as do something else)

인사도 할 겸 = to say hi (to someone while I am there)

가격도 알아볼 겸 = to check the prices as well (while I am there doing something else)

2.

홍대에 갈 수도 있어요. = I might go to Hongdae.

친구를 만날 수도 있어요. = I might meet a friend.

제 친구가 알 수도 있어요. = (I do not know, but) My friend might know.

제 친구를 알 수도 있어요. = You might know my friend.

다시 올 수도 있어요. = I might come back again.

Expansion & Variation Practice with Key Sentence (2)

0. Original Sentence:

내일 다시 오거나, 아니면 다른 사람에게 부탁할게요.

= I will either come again tomorrow or ask someone else.

1.

내일 다시 오거나 = come again tomorrow or

친구를 만나거나 = meet a friend or

친구한테 물어보거나 = ask a friend or

여기에서 기다리거나 = wait here or

2.

아니면 다른 사람에게 부탁할게요. = or I will ask someone else.

아니면 나중에 다시 할게요. = or I will do it again later.

아니면 그냥 제가 할게요. = or I will just do it myself.

아니면 여기에 있을 수도 있어요. = or it might be here.

Track 39

Expansion & Variation Practice with Key Sentence (3)

0. Original Sentence:

그러니까, 누구하고 같이 갈 거라고요?

= So I mean, who did you say you were going to go with?

1.

그러니까, 누구하고 갈 거예요? = So, who are you going to go with?

그러니까 이거 뭐예요? = I mean, what is this?

by Expressing Doubts, Abilities, and Happenings

그러니까 혼자 왔다고요? = You mean you came here alone?

그러니까 제가 안 했어요. = What I am saying is, I did not do it.

2.

누구하고 같이 갈 거라고요?

= You said you were going to go with who? / Again, who are you going with?

언제 할 거라고요?

= You said you were going to do it when? / Again, when are you going to do it?

이게 뭐라고요?

= What did you say this was? / Again, what is this?

Track 39

128

Sample Dialogue

에밀리: 한국 드라마 보는 거 좋아해요?

캐시: 아니요. 에밀리 씨는 좋아해요?

에밀리: 네. 한국어 공부도 할 겸 자주 봐요.
그럼 캐시 씨는 한국어 공부 어떻게
해요?

캐시: 저는 유튜브 영상 보거나 아니면
팟캐스트 많이 들어요.

Emily: Do you like watching Korean dramas?

Cassie: No. Do you?

Emily: Yes. I often watch them so I can also learn Korean. So then how do you study Korean?

Cassie: I watch YouTube videos or listen to lots of podcasts.

by Expressing Doubts, Abilities, and Happenings

Check the answers on **p.210**

✎ *Exercises for Lesson* **20**

Translate each phrase or sentence into Korean and then write it on the lines provided below.

1. I mean, what is this?

....

2. You said you were going to go with who?

....

3. or I will ask someone else.

....

4. (I do not know, but) My friend might know.

....

5. to say hi (to someone while I am here)

....

DAKGALBI RECIPE
(닭갈비)

When I first moved to Korea, one of the first dishes that really stood out to me was dakgalbi (닭갈비). For those who may not know what it is, the dish consists of marinated chicken stir-fried with sweet potatoes (고구마), cabbage (양배추), perilla leaves (깻잎), tteok (떡, or rice cakes), and sometimes various other ingredients, with gochujang (고추장) as a base sauce. Many people wrap the chicken and vegetables in lettuce and perilla leaves to eat. If you are still hungry after eating most of the stir-fried food, you can add rice to the pan, mix it with whatever is left over, and top it with some seaweed to make fried rice. To be honest, finishing the meal in this way is almost like having a second course it tastes so good!

The first time my dad came to visit me in Korea, I took him to a dakgalbi restaurant and he absolutely loved it. He said it was the best thing he had during his trip! Even after visiting a second time, dakgalbi was at the top of the list of things he wanted to eat. Later on, he even asked for the recipe so he could make it at home.

Did you know that dakgalbi wasn't always a main dish here in Korea? It originated in Chuncheon in the 1960s as anju (안주), a dish that is served with alcohol. Restaurants used grilled pieces of chicken to replace some of the more expensive grilled meat (구이). During the 70's, the dish became very popular with students and those in the military, and became known as the "commoners' galbi".

Now, just like I did with my father, I am going to share with you a quick recipe for dakgalbi so you can make it in your own home.

Here is what you will need:

250g Boneless Chicken Pieces

150g Rice Cakes (tteokbokki rice cakes)

¼ Onion, chopped

¼ Sweet Potato, thinly sliced

½ (10cm) Green Onion, thickly sliced

10 Sesame Leaves, roughly chopped

100g Cabbage, roughly chopped

Cooking Oil to put into the pan for cooking

Salt and Pepper

For the sauce:

3 Tablespoons Red Pepper Paste

1 ½ Tablespoons Red Pepper/Chilli Powder

1 Tablespoon Mirim (Cooking Wine)

1 Tablespoon Minced Garlic

1 Teaspoon Minced Ginger

1 ½ ~ 2 Tablespoons Sugar

2 Tablespoons Soy Sauce

1 Teaspoon Sesame Oil

Directions:

Cut the chicken into small bite-sized pieces.

Mix the chicken with the sauce and let sit for about 30 minutes (Don't use all of the sauce now as you will use some of it later).

Cut the spring onions, sweet potatoes, cabbage, and onions.

For the sesame leaves, fold them in half and cut them to make thin strips.

Pour the cooking oil into a pan and begin cooking the chicken and sweet potatoes.

When the chicken is almost done, add the other vegetables and rice cakes.

Add the rest of the sauce you made and mix well.

That's all it takes to make your own dakgalbi at home! It may seem like a bit of work, but it is well worth it. If you go to a restaurant and eat dakgalbi, they tend to serve fried rice afterwards. If you would like to do that, take some rice and seaweed and mix your leftovers in a pan. Add a bit of homemade sauce and let it cook for a bit. Then enjoy!

Written by Johnny Bland

LESSON 21

Passive Voice (Part 1)

-이/히/리/기-, -아/어/여지다

Track 41

In this lesson, let's take a look at how to make sentences in the passive voice.

What is Passive Voice?

Passive voice is a form of sentence in which the focus is on the recipient of an action, rather than the subject. For example, when you *make* something, that something is *made* by you. When you recommend a book to someone, the book *is recommended* by you. That is passive voice, and the opposite of passive voice is active voice.

Something that is done, sold, bought, etc. by someone are all being talked about in the passive voice. Active voice is, "I do something."

How to Make Passive Voice Sentences in Korean

In English, to make passive voice you can change the verb into its "past participle" form and add it after the BE verb, but in Korean you need to conjugate the verb in the "passive voice" form by adding a suffix or a verb ending.

There are two ways to make passive voice in Korean.

Verb stem + **-이/히/리/기-**

Verb stem + **-아/어/여지다**

Passive voice in English and passive voice in Korean are a little different; just by adding one of these suffixes to the verb stem, the "passive voice" verb itself can actually work like a stand-alone active verb in Korean.

Meanings

In English, passive voice sentences are just "passive voice" sentences. However, in Korean, the verbs take on the meaning of "can/to be possible/to be doable/would" as well. Therefore, it is almost even incorrect to call it the "passive voice" in this case. For Part 1, let's look at the "passive voice" meaning of these verb endings.

Track 41

Difference Between -아/어/여지다 and -이/히/리/기-

There is no clear rule about which verb stem should be followed by -아/어/여지다 and which should be followed by -이/히/리/기-. Native speakers usually determine which ending to use based on their previous experience of hearing the words being used. Using and hearing these over and over will help you determine how to use them.

Conjugation Rule #1: Verb stem + -아/어/여지다

In Level 4 Lesson 28, we introduced -아/어/여지다 as the conjugation for changing an adjective into the "to become + adjective" form, but when you use -아/어/여지다 with ACTION verbs, the verbs take on the passive voice meaning.

1. Change the verb into the present tense.
2. Drop -(아/어/여)요.
3. Add -(아/어/여)지다.

Example 1

자르다 = to cut

자르다 is a "르 irregular" verb, so it is conjugated to 잘라요 in the present tense. You drop -요 and add -지다, and you have 잘라지다.

Track 41

자르다 → 잘라(요) → 잘라지다 = to get cut (by a knife or scissors)

Example 2

주다 = to give
주다 → 주어(요) → 주어지다 = to be given

Example 3

보내다 = to send
보내다 → 보내(요) → 보내지다 = to be sent

Conjugation Rule #2: Verb stem + -이/히/리/기-

There is no 'single' rule that determines which verb stem or letter is followed by which among 이, 히, 리 and 기, but the general rule is as follows:

(1) -이-

When the dictionary form of the verb ends in -ㅎ다, -이- is added to the verb ending and it is changed to -ㅎ이다.

Ex)
놓다 (to put down) → 놓이다 (to be put down)
쌓다 (to pile up) → 쌓이다 (to be piled up)

(2) -히-

When the dictionary form of the verb ends in -ㄱ다, -ㄷ다 or -ㅂ다, -히- is added to the verb ending and it is changed to -ㄱ히다, -ㄷ히다 or -ㅂ히다.

Ex)
먹다 (to eat) → 먹히다 (to be eaten)
닫다 (to close) → 닫히다 (to get closed)
잡다 (to catch) → 잡히다 (to get caught)

(3) -리-

When the dictionary form of the verb ends in -ㄹ다, -리- is added to the verb ending and it is changed to -ㄹ리다.

Ex)

밀다 (to push) → 밀리다 (to be pushed)

풀다 (to untie) → 풀리다 (to come untied)

(4) -기-

When the dictionary form of the verb ends in -ㄴ다, ㅁ다, ㅅ다 or ㅊ다, -기- is added to the verb ending and it is changed to -ㄴ기다, -ㅁ기다, -ㅅ기다 or -ㅊ기다.

Ex)

안다 (to hug) → 안기다 (to be hugged)

담다 (to put something in a basket/bag) → 담기다 (to be put into a basket/bag)

씻다 (to wash) → 씻기다 (to be washed)

쫓다 (to chase) → 쫓기다 (to be chased)

Track 41

-이/히/리/기- + -아/어/여지다 (Double Passive Voice)

Sometimes, these two types of verb endings are used TOGETHER in one verb.

Ex)

놓다 → 놓이다 → 놓여지다

안다 → 안기다 → 안겨지다

There is no 'standard' explanation, but this is most likely because people want to clarify and emphasize the passive voice of the verb. Some grammarians argue that this 'double passive voice' is incorrect, but it is already being widely used.

Passive Voice of 하다 Verbs

하다 verbs are combinations of other nouns and 하다, such as 이용하다 (to use), 연구하다 (to research), etc. In order to change these 하다 verbs into the passive voice, you need to change 하다 to 되다.

이용하다 → 이용되다 (to be used)
연구하다 → 연구되다 (to be researched)

Even for 하다/되다, double passive voice is often used.

이용되다 = 이용되어지다
연구되다 = 연구되어지다

Track 41

This is Part 1 of the Passive Voice lesson. In Part 2, we will look at how passive voice in Korean takes on the meaning of "possibility" or "capability".

Sample Dialogue

🎙️ Track 42

민주: 왜 이렇게 뛰어와요? 누구한테 쫓기고 있어요? 운동화 끈도 풀렸어요.

석진: 민주 씨가 급한 일이라고 빨리 오라고 했잖아요.

민주: 제가요?

Minjoo: Why did you run? Are you being chased by someone? Your shoelaces came undone, too.

Seokjin: You said it was urgent and to come quickly.

Minjoo: I did?

✎ Exercises for Lesson 21

Change the following words to the passive form.

1. 이용하다 (to use) →

2. 보내다 (to send) →

3. 먹다 (to eat) →

4. 잡다 (to catch) →

5. 풀다 (to untie, to solve) →

Check the answers on **p.210**

by Expressing Doubts, Abilities, and Happenings

LESSON 22

Word Builder 11

무 (無)

Track 43

Word Builder lessons are designed to help you understand how to expand your vocabulary by learning and understanding some common and basic building blocks of Korean words. The words and letters introduced through Word Builder lessons are not necessarily all Chinese characters, or 한자. Though many of them are based on Chinese characters, the meanings can be different from modern-day Chinese. Your goal through these lessons is to understand how words are formed and then remember the keywords in Korean to expand your Korean vocabulary from there. You certainly do not have to memorize the Hanja characters, but if you want to, feel free!

Today's keyword element is 무.

The Chinese character for this is 無.

The word 무 is related to "none", "nothing", and "non-existence".

무 (none) + 공해 (pollution) = 무공해 無公害 = pollution-free, clean

144

무 (none) + 료 (fee) = 무료 無料 = free of charge

Related Vocabulary

공짜 空- = free

* 짜 is not based on a Chinese character.

요금 料金 = fee

* 料 is pronounced as 요 when it comes at the beginning of a word.

무 (none) + 시 (to see) = 무시 無視 = to overlook, to neglect, to disregard

Related Vocabulary

시력 視力 = eyesight

Track 43

Ex)

무시하지 마세요. = Don't ignore me.

무 (none) + 책임 (responsibility) = 무책임 無責任 = irresponsibility

무 (none) + 조건 (condition) = 무조건 無條件 = unconditionally

무 (none) + 죄 (sin, guilt) = 무죄 無罪 = innocent, not guilty

Related Vocabulary

유죄 有罪 = guilty

무 (none) + 능력 (ability) = 무능력 無能力 = incapability, incompetence

Related Vocabulary

무능하다 無能-- = to be incompetent

145

유능하다 有能-- = to be competent

무 (none) + 한 (limit) = 무한 無限 = infinite, limitless

무 (none) + 적 (enemy) = 무적 無敵 = unbeatable, invincible

무 (none) + 사고 (accident) = 무사고 無事故 = no accident

무 (none) + 관심 (interest) = 무관심 無關心 = indifference, showing no interest

무 (none) + 명 (name) = 무명 無名 = not popular, unknown

Related Vocabulary

이름 = name

* 이름 is a native Korean word.

성명 姓名 = full name (lit. surname and name)

무 (none) + 인 (person) = 무인 無人 = unmanned, uninhabited

Related Vocabulary

무인도 無人島 = uninhabited island

Sample Dialogue

Track 44

리포터: 이번 영화에서 어떤 역할을
맡았어요?

진영: 무명 배우 역할을 맡았어요.

리포터: 진영 씨는 무명 시절에 어땠어요?

진영: 사람들이 저를 무시한다고
생각했어요. 그래서 촬영장 구석에서
많이 울었어요.

Reporter: What role did you play in this movie?

Jinyoung: I played the part of the unknown actor.

*Reporter: How were your days as an unknown
actor?*

*Jinyoung: I thought people were ignoring me. So I
cried a lot in the corners on set.*

147

by Expressing Doubts, Abilities, and Happenings

✎ Exercises for Lesson 22

Fill in the blanks with the appropriate Sino-Korean word from the lesson.

1. The key word element (   ) is related to "none", "nothing", and "non-existence".

2. (   ) = innocent, not guilty

3. (   ) = unmanned, uninhabited

4. (   ) = incapability, incompetence

5. (   ) = irresponsibility

Check the answers on **p.210**

148

LESSON **23**

Passive Voice (Part 2)

-이/히/리/기-, -아/어/여지다

Track
45

Welcome to Part 2 of the Passive Voice lesson! In Part 1, we learned how sentences in the passive voice are generally made. In this part, let's take a look at how the passive voice in English and in Korean are different, as well as some more example sentences.

Let's review a little bit first.

Suffixes for passive voice in Korean:
Verb stem + **-이/히/리/기-**
Verb stem + **-아/어/여지다**

Again, there is no fixed rule for which verb stem should be followed by one of the -이/히/리/기- suffixes and which should be followed by -아/어/여지다. Some verbs even have an identical meaning when followed by either of these two grammar points!

by Expressing Doubts, Abilities, and Happenings

Ex)

자르다 = to cut

\+ -이/히/리/기- → 잘리다 = to be cut

\+ -아/어/여지다 → 잘라지다 = to be cut

풀다 = to untie, to solve

\+ -이/히/리/기- → 풀리다 = to come untied, to be solved

\+ -아/어/여지다 → 풀어지다 = to come untied, to be solved

Another Meaning for Passive Voice Sentences in Korean

Track 45

In Korean, in addition to the meaning of an action "being done", the meaning of "possibility" or "capability" is also very commonly used with passive voice sentences (The basic idea is that, when you do something, if something gets done, it is doable. If something does not get done when you do or try to do it, it is not doable or not possible to do).

This meaning of "possibility" or "capability" does not signify YOUR ability or capability so much as it does the general "possibility" of that certain action being done.

Examples

만들다 is "to make", and when you say 만들어지다, in the standard passive voice sense, it would mean "to be made." However, 만들어지다 can not only mean "to be made", but it can also mean "can be made".

Ex)

이 핸드폰은 중국에서 만들어져요.

= This cell phone is made in China.

150

케이크를 예쁘게 만들고 싶은데, 예쁘게 안 만들어져요.

= I want to make this cake in a pretty shape, but I cannot make it pretty.

In the 2nd example sentence, you can see that the person is NOT directly saying that he or she can NOT make a pretty cake, but that the cake does NOT get made in a pretty shape.

If you just say, "예쁘게 못 만들어요", it might mean that you lack the ability to make it pretty.

More Examples

이거 안 잘라져요.

= This does not get cut.

= I cannot cut it. (more accurate)

Track 45

안 들려요.

= It is not heard.

= I cannot hear you. (more accurate)

안 보여요.

= It is not seen.

= I cannot see it.

하다 vs. 되다

Since the passive voice represents "possibility" or "capability", the passive voice form of 하다, which is 되다, takes on the meaning of "can" as well.

하다 = to do (active voice)

151

되다 = to be done, to get done (passive voice)

되다 = can be done, can do (possibility/capability)

Ex)

이거 안 돼요.

= This does not get done.

= I cannot do this. (more accurate)

= I cannot seem to do it. (more accurate)

이해가 안 돼요.

= Understanding is not done.

= It is not understood.

= I cannot understand. (more accurate)

= I do not understand. (more accurate)

Track 45

More Examples With 되다

From there, we can create additional patterns with 되다.

Originally, 되다 means "to be done", but it can also mean things like:

- can be served

- to be available

- can be spoken

- can be done

- can be made

- can be finished

- etc.

Ex)

여기 김밥 돼요?

= Do you have/serve gimbap here?

영어가 안 돼서 걱정이에요.

= I am worried because I cannot speak English.

오늘 안에 돼요?

= Can you finish it today?

So how often does the passive voice take on the meaning of "possibility"?

Track 45

Through Part 1 and 2 of this lesson, we have looked at how passive voice sentences are formed and used. First, you need to figure out (by being exposed to a lot of Korean sentences or by memorizing the suffixes that go with each verb) which of the endings is used in the passive voice form. Also, you need to tell from the context of the sentence whether the verb is used in the original "passive" voice form or in the sense of "possibility/capability".

Often times, though, sentences that would certainly be in the passive voice are written in the active voice in Korean. This is because, in English, you use the passive voice in order to NOT show the subject of a certain action in a sentence; in Korean, you can easily drop the subject, so you do not have to worry about it as much.

For example, when you say, "This was made in Korea", who are you referring to? Who made it? Do you know? Probably not. Therefore, in English, you just say that "it" was made in Korea. In Korean, you do not have to worry about the subject of the verb, so you can just use the active voice form and say, "한국에서 만든 거예요" or "한국에서 만들었어요." In these two sentences, the verbs are in the active voice, but no one asks, "So who made it?" as it is understood that, "It was made (by somebody) in Korea."

153

Sample Dialogue

Track
46

주연: 어? 핸드폰이 갑자기 꺼졌어요.

경화: 배터리 없어요?

주연: 아니요. 고장 난 것 같아요. 아예 안 켜져요.

Jooyeon: Huh? My phone died all of a sudden.

Kyung-hwa: Is the battery dead?

Jooyeon: No. I think it's broken. It won't turn on at all.

154

✎ Exercises for Lesson **23**

Check the answers on **p.210**

Fill in the blanks by using passive voice.

1. 케이크를 예쁘게 만들고 싶은데, 예쁘게 ( ).

  = I want to make this cake in a pretty shape, but I cannot make it pretty.

2. 이거 ( ).

  = This does not get cut.

  = I cannot cut it. (more accurate)

3. ( ).

  = It is not heard.

  = I cannot hear you. (more accurate)

4. ( ).

  = It is not seen.

  = I cannot see it.

5. 이해가 ( ).

  = Understanding is not done.

  = It is not understood.

  = I cannot understand. (more accurate)

  = I do not understand. (more accurate)

by **Expressing Doubts, Abilities, and Happenings**

LESSON 24

I DID do it, but …, I DO like it, but …

-기는 하다

Track 47

When you want to emphasize an action or state in English, you either do it by adding more stress to the verb in the intonation, or by adding the word "do" in front of the verb.

Example #1
A: It is not easy.
B: No, it IS easy!

Example #2
A: Why did not you go there?
B: I DID go, but I came back early.

Example #3
A: Do you think you can do it?
B: Well, I COULD do it, but I do not want to do it.

In this lesson, let's take a look at how to express this emphasis in Korean.

The simplest way to do this is by changing the intonation.

A: 왜 안 했어요? = Why did not you do it?

B: 했어요! = I DID do it!

This example is when you are simply disagreeing with the other person and presenting a different fact.

If you want to add some conditions or premises to your sentence and say, "I did do it, but..." or "I do like it, but...", you need to use a different verb ending.

Example #1

A: So you did not even do it?

B: I did!! I DID do it, but I had some help.

Track 47

Example #2

A: Can you do it?

B: I COULD do it, but I do not want to do it.

Now let's look at how to express these in Korean.

The key is **-기는**. This is the noun form -기 plus the topic marker -는. The topic marker is used to show contrast.

Example #1

갔어요. = I went (there).

 → 가기는 갔어요. = I DID go (there) but...

If you do not want to repeat the 가다 verb, you can change it to 하다.

→ 가기는 했어요. = I DID go (there) but...

→ 가기는 갔는데, 일찍 왔어요. = I DID go there, but I came back early.

→ 가기는 갈 거예요. = I WILL go, but... (+ other premises)

Example #2

봤어요. = I saw (it).

→ 보기는 봤어요. = I DID see (it) but...

→ 보기는 했어요. = I DID see (it) but...

→ 보기는 봤는데 기억이 안 나요. = I DID see it, but I do not remember.

"봤어요. 그런데..." is changed to 봤는데.

How to Say "I COULD do it but..."

Track
47

To say that you can do something, you use the structure -(으)ㄹ 수 있다. Here, -(으)ㄹ 수 is a Noun Group that literally means "a method for doing something" or "possibility/ability". Therefore, you can JUST use the topic marker without having to change it again into the noun form. It is already a noun.

Example

할 수 있어요. = I can do (it).

→ 할 수는 있어요. = I COULD do it, but...

→ 할 수는 있는데, 안 하고 싶어요. = I COULD do it, but I do not want to.

→ 할 수는 있는데, 안 해 줄 거예요. = I COULD do it, but I am not going to do it for you.

→ 할 수는 있는데, 조건이 있어요. = I COULD do it, but there is a condition.

→ 할 수는 있는데, 시간이 걸려요. = I COULD do it, but it will take some time.

158

Sample Sentences

어제 친구를 만나기는 했는데, 금방 헤어졌어요.

= I DID meet a friend yesterday, but we parted soon after.

> * "어제 친구를 만났는데, 금방 헤어졌어요" means that you are not upset and are just stating the facts. If you say the one above, though, you are showing that you are upset.

시간 맞춰서 도착하기는 했는데, 준비를 못 했어요.

= I DID manage to get there on time, but I could not prepare (it).

> * Again, with this phrase you are showing emphasis that you got there on time but just could not prepare for something in a timely manner.

읽기는 읽었는데 이해가 안 돼요.

= I DID read it, but I do not understand it.

Track 47

좋기는 좋은데, 너무 비싸요.

= It IS good, but it is too expensive.

맛있기는 맛있는데, 좀 짜요.

= It IS delicious, but it is a bit salty.

Sample Dialogue

Track
48

지민: 경화 씨, 안녕하세요. 아침 먹었어요?
저 지금 나가서 먹을 거 사 오려고
하는데.

경화: 아침 먹기는 먹었는데, 또 먹을래요.
제 것도 부탁할게요.

지민: 네. 뭐 사 올까요?

Jimin: Hello, Kyung-hwa. Did you have breakfast?
I was about to go out and bring back
something to eat.

Kyung-hwa: I did have breakfast, but I'll eat again.
Get me something, too.

Jimin: Sure. What would you like?

✏ Exercises for Lesson 24

Translate each phrase into Korean by using -기는 *and write it in the space provided.*

1. It IS delicious, but it is a bit salty.

....

2. It IS good, but it is too expensive.

....

3. I DID see it, but I do not remember.

....

4. I DID read it, but I do not understand it.

....

5. I DID meet a friend yesterday, but we parted soon after.

....

Check the answers on **p.211**

by **Expressing Doubts, Abilities, and Happenings**

LESSON 25

To be easy/difficult to + verb

-기 쉽다/어렵다

Track 49

In this lesson, let's take a look at how to say that something is easy or difficult to do. To say this, you need to use the noun form of verbs, ending with -기.

To be easy to + Verb = -기 쉽다

Ex)

하기 쉽다 = to be easy to do

잊기 쉽다 = to be easy to forget

먹기 쉽다 = to be easy to eat

사기 쉽다 = to be easy to buy

To be difficult to + Verb = -기 어렵다

Ex)

하기 어렵다 = to be difficult to do

찾기 어렵다 = to be difficult to find

"Verb stem + -기" is a noun form; in principle, there has to be a marker after it, but in the forms above, the marker is dropped.

Q: Which markers were dropped?
A: It depends on the context, but -기 쉽다/어렵다 can be written either as -기에 쉽다/어렵다 or -기가 쉽다/어렵다.

-기에 쉽다/어렵다

When you use the marker -에, it means that something is easy/difficult FOR + Verb-ing.

-기가 쉽다/어렵다

When you use the marker -가, it means that DOING something is easy/difficult.

Let's look at some examples.

Track 49

Example #1

제 이름은 발음하기(가) 어려워요.

= My name is difficult to pronounce.

= As for my name, pronouncing it is difficult.

Example #2

이건 만들기(가) 어려워요.

= This is difficult to make.

= As for this, making it is difficult.

Example #3

이건 어린이가 사용하기(에) 어려워요.

= This is difficult for a child to use.

= Using this is difficult for a child.

* In this example, since the subject of the verb **사용하다** is **어린이** and **어린이** is followed by **-가**, the subject marker, it sounds rather repetitive to use **-가** again, so in this kind of sentence, people tend to use **-에** instead of **-가** before **쉬워요/어려워요**.

Example #4

사용하기가 쉬워요.

= It is easy to use.

Track 49

사용하기에 쉬워요.

= Using it is easy.

* In this case, **-가 쉬워요** and **-에 쉬워요** both work because the sentences are short.

In all of the above sentences, you can drop -가 or -에 from -기가 or -기에.

1. 제 이름은 발음하기가 어려워요.

　　→　제 이름은 발음하기 어려워요.

2. 이건 만들기가 어려워요.

　　→　이건 만들기 어려워요.

3. 이건 어린이가 사용하기에 어려워요.

    → 이건 어린이가 사용하기 어려워요.

4. 사용하기가 쉬워요.

    → 사용하기 쉬워요.

5. 사용하기에 쉬워요.

    → 사용하기 쉬워요.

Other words can also be used with "Verb stem + -기(가/에)".

Examples

Track 49

-기(가) 편리하다 / -기(에) 편리하다

= to be convenient to + Verb / to be convenient for + Verb-ing

-기(가) 좋다 / -기(에) 좋다

= to be good to + Verb / to be good for + Verb-ing

-기(가) 불편하다 / -기(에) 불편하다

= to be inconvenient to + Verb / to be inconvenient for + Verb-ing

Sample Dialogue

Track
50

경화: 비빔밥을 젓가락으로 먹어요?

캐시: 네.

경화: 왜요? 비빔밥은 젓가락으로 먹기
      어렵잖아요.

캐시: 아니에요. 전혀 어렵지 않아요.

Kyung-hwa: You eat bibimbap with chopsticks?

Cassie: Yeah.

Kyung-hwa: Why? It's hard to eat bibimbap with
           chopsticks.

Cassie: No, it's not hard at all.

✏ Exercises for Lesson 25

Write the following sentences in Korean using -기(가) or -기(에).

1. It is easy to use.

....

2. As for this, making it is difficult.

....

3. This is difficult for a child to use.

....

4. As for my name, pronouncing it is difficult.

....

Check the answers on **p.211**

167

LESSON 26

To know/think that someone has done/will do something

-(으)ㄴ/ㄹ 줄 알다

Track
51

In this lesson, let's take a look at how to say things like, "I thought you would do it", "I did not think you would do it", "I thought I was…", etc.

The key structure used for this is **-(으)ㄴ/ㄹ 줄 알다**.

-(으)ㄴ 줄 알다 = to know/think that someone has done something
-(으)ㄹ 줄 알다 = to know/think that someone will do something
* Note that -(으)ㄴ is usually associated with the past tense and -(으)ㄹ is usually used associated with the future tense.

Even though -(으)ㄴ/ㄹ 줄 알다 could be used in present tense or future tense sentences, this grammar point is mostly used in the past tense. That means the verb 알다 is mostly used in the form, 알았어요.

168

Ex)

비가 올 줄 알았어요.

= I knew it was going to rain.

= I thought it was going to rain.

사람이 많을 줄 알았어요.

= I knew there would be a lot of people.

= I thought there would be a lot of people.

How to Tell Whether It Means "I knew" or "I thought"?

The meanings can be very different between, "I knew you would like it" and "I thought you would like it". The written form for both of these in Korean is the same, but the intonation in spoken Korean is different. When you have more stress on the verb 알다, it means "I knew" and when the stress is on the -(으)ㄴ/ㄹ 줄 part, it means "I thought."

Track 51

Ex)

제가 말할 줄 알았어요?

(with emphasis on 알았어요?) = Did you know that I would tell you?

(with emphasis on 말할 줄) = Did you think that I would tell you?

Ex)

어디로 갈 줄 알았어요?

(with emphasis on 알았어요?) = Did you know where he/she/they would go?

(with emphasis on 어디로) = Where did you think he/she/they would go?

Difference Between -(으)ㄴ 줄 알다 and -(으)ㄹ 줄 알다

Basically -(으)ㄴ 줄 알다 expresses your knowledge or assumption about a PAST ACTION or a PRESENT STATE, whereas -(으)ㄹ 줄 알다 expresses your knowledge or assumption about a FUTURE action or state. To express your knowledge or assumption about a PRESENT ACTION, you need to use -는 줄 알다.

예쁜 줄 알다

= (with emphasis on 알다) to know that something/someone is pretty

= (with emphasis on 예쁜 줄) to think that something/someone is pretty

Track 51

> **Ex)**
> 제 친구는 자기가 세상에서 제일 예쁜 줄 알아요.
> = My friend thinks that she is the prettiest in the world.

간 줄 알다

= (with emphasis on 알다) = to know that someone has gone somewhere

= (with emphasis on 간 줄) = to think that someone has gone somewhere

> **Ex)**
> 제가 학교에 간 줄 알았어요?
> = (with emphasis on 알았어요?) = Did you know that I had gone to school?
> = (with emphasis on 간 줄) = Did you think that I had gone to school?

How to Say "I did not know I would..." and "I did not think I would..."

There are two ways to make the -(으)ㄹ 줄 알았어요 a negative sentence. One is to change 알았어요 to 몰랐어요. The other is to add 안 to the verb that comes before -(으)ㄹ 줄 알았어요.

Ex)

오늘 눈이 올 줄 알았어요.

= I knew it would snow today.

= I thought it would snow today.

→ 오늘 눈이 올 줄 몰랐어요.

= I did not know it would snow today.

→ 오늘 눈이 안 올 줄 알았어요.

= I thought it would not snow today.

Sample Sentences

Track 51

이게 여기 있을 줄 몰랐어요.

= I did not know it would be here.

저는 경화 씨도 온 줄 알았어요.

= I thought Kyung-hwa also came. / I knew kyung-hwa also came.

이렇게 비싼 줄 몰랐어요.

= I did not know it was this expensive.

저는 안 어려울 줄 알았어요.

= I thought it would not be difficult. / I knew it would not be difficult.

제가 뭐라고 할 줄 알았어요?

= What did you think I would say? / Did you know what I would say?

171

by Expressing Doubts, Abilities, and Happenings

Sample Dialogue

Track 52

현무: 혜진 씨한테 약속 시간 바뀌었다고 방금 문자 보냈어요.

나래: 아! 제가 이미 보냈는데.

현무: 아, 정말요? 나래 씨가 보낸 줄 몰랐어요. 아직 말 안 한 줄 알았어요.

Hyunmoo: I just sent a message to Hyejin that the time has changed.

Narae: Ah! I already sent her a message.

Hyunmoo: Oh really? I didn't know you had already sent it. I thought you hadn't said anything yet.

✏ Exercises for Lesson 26

Translate each sentence into Korean using -(으)ㄴ/ㄹ 줄 알았어요/몰랐어요.

1. I did not know it would be here.

....

2. I thought Kyung-hwa also came.

....

3. I thought it would not be difficult.

....

4. What did you think I would say?

....

5. I did not know it was this expensive.

....

Check the answers on **p.211**

by Expressing Doubts, Abilities, and Happenings

LESSON 27

Can, To be able to, To know how to

-(으)ㄹ 수 있다, -(으)ㄹ 줄 알다

Track 53

In the previous lesson, we learned how to use -(으)ㄹ 줄 알다 to say "to think/know that something will happen". This sentence ending can be also used to express "can", "to be able to", or "to know how to". The same meaning can also be expressed through -(으)ㄹ 수 있다; through this lesson, let's find out how these two verb endings are used similarly or differently to express "can" or "to be able to".

-(으)ㄹ 수 있다

This ending was introduced in Level 2 Lesson 17. This is the basic way to say "can" or "to be able to". 수 basically means "possibility" or "method".

Ex)

이거 할 수 있어요? = Can you do this?

언제 올 수 있어요? = When can you come?

여기에서 뭐 살 수 있어요? = What can I buy (it) here?

174

How to Say "can NOT"

If you want to say "can NOT", you can change 있다 to 없다 or add 못 to the sentence.

Ex)

갈 수 없어요. = I cannot go.

못 가요. = I cannot go.

-(으)ㄹ 줄 알다

This structure was introduced in the previous lesson as a sentence ending that means "to think/know that something will happen/be in a certain state". When you are talking about "knowing how to do something" or "being able to do something", 줄 here means "method" or "how".

Track 53

-(으)ㄹ 줄 = how/method

알다 = to know

-(으)ㄹ 줄 알다 = to know how to + Verb / to be able to + Verb

Ex)

운전 할 줄 알아요?

= Do you know how to drive?

= Can you drive?

* "운전 할 수 있어요?" has the same meaning.

김치 만들 줄 알아요?

= Do you know how to make kimchi?

= Can you make kimchi?

175

영어 할 줄 알아요?

= Do you (know how to) speak English?

= Can you speak English?

How to Say "can NOT"

If you want to say "can NOT", you need to change 알다 to 모르다. 모르다 means "to not know".

Ex)

영어 할 줄 알아요? = Can you speak English?

영어 할 줄 몰라요. = I do not know how to speak English.

김치 만들 줄 알아요? = Can you make kimchi?

김치 만들 줄 몰라요. = I do not know how to make kimchi.

Track 53

운전 할 줄 알아요? = Can you drive?

운전 할 줄 몰라요. = I do not know how to drive.

Difference Between -(으)ㄹ 수 있다 and -(으)ㄹ 줄 알다

-(으)ㄹ 수 있다 is the basic way to say "can" or "to be able to", so it usually refers to one's actual "capability" of doing something. On the other hand, -(으)ㄹ 줄 알다 means that you know how to do something, and you can do it, but in most cases, you have LEARNED how to do it. Therefore there are some things that you CAN (-을 수 있다) do (potentially), but can NOT do it yet because you still do not know how to do it.

Ex)

아직 할 줄 몰라요. 그런데 할 수 있어요.

176

= I do not know how to do it yet. (I cannot do it yet.) But I am able to do it.

Sample Sentences

이거 할 줄 알아요?

= Do you know how to do this?

= 이거 할 수 있어요?

저는 영어 할 줄 몰라요.

= I do not speak English.

= I do not know how to speak English.

= I cannot speak English.

    * If you know how to speak English, but cannot speak English at that moment, you would say, "영어 못 해요. = I cannot speak English (now)."

그거 한국어로 말할 수 있어요?

= Can you say that in Korean?

    * You would use this if you know they can speak in Korean, but are asking them to say what they said again in Korean.

Track 53

그거 한국어로 말할 줄 알아요?

= Do you know how to say that in Korean?

자전거 탈 줄 알아요?

= Do you know how to ride a bike?

= Can you ride a bike?

자전거 탈 수 있어요?

= Can you ride a bike?

= Can you ride a bike (now/like that)?

How to Tell Which Meaning -(으)ㄹ 줄 알다 Takes

-(으)ㄹ 줄 알다 can mean either "to know how to" and "to know/think that something will happen". There is no certain rule for this, but you can usually figure it out by context.

Examples

제가 올 줄 알았어요?

In the example above, if you interpret it as, "Did I know how to come here?", it is a bit weird. So you know it SHOULD mean, "Did you know I would come here?" or "Did you think I would come here?"

Track 53

이거 만들 줄 알아요?

In the example above, if you interpret it as, "Do you think…" or "Do you know…", you do not have enough information to figure out who's going to make "this". The meaning is usually not commonly used in the present tense, so you know it is easier to understand it as a question asking, "Do you know how to make this?"

Sample Dialogue

Track 54

소영: 제가 직접 만든 떡이에요. 한번 드셔
보세요.

경은: 네? 방금 직접 만들었다고 했어요? 소영
씨는 떡도 만들 줄 알아요?

소영: 네. 떡 만들기 어렵지 않아요.

Soyoung: I made this rice cake myself. Try it.

*Kyeong-eun: Huh? Did you just say that you made
it yourself? You know how to make rice
cakes?*

Soyoung: Yes. Rice cakes aren't hard to make.

by Expressing Doubts, Abilities, and Happenings

✐ Exercises for Lesson **27**

Rewrite the following sentences using -(으)ㄹ 줄 알아요.

1. 운전 할 수 있어요?　　→

2. 자전거 탈 수 있어요?　　→

3. 이거 할 수 있어요?　　→

4. 김치 만들 수 있어요?　　→

5. 한국어로 말할 수 있어요?　　→

Check the answers on **p.211**

LESSON 28

It depends …

-에 따라 달라요

In this lesson, let's look at how to say "It depends on…" or just "It depends…" in Korean.

🎙
Track 55

The verb "to depend" is literally translated as 의지하다 or 의존하다, but this is only when you are talking about actually being "dependent" on someone about a certain matter.

For example, if you want to say something like, "Don't depend on your parents", you can use the verb 의지하다 or 의존하다 and say, "부모님한테 의지하지 마세요."

However, when you want to say, "It depends on the situation", "It depends on the person", or "It depends on how soon you finish this", you need to use the structure -에 따라 다르다 or -마다 다르다.

-에 따라 다르다

-에 따라 means "according to", "in compliance with", or "in accordance with". 다르다 means "to be different". Literally, this structure means, "It changes/becomes different in accordance with (something)."

Sample Sentences

때에 따라 달라요.

= It depends on the time.

= It depends on when it is.

상황에 따라 달라요.

= It depends on the situation.

사람에 따라 달라요.

= It depends on the person.

You can also say -에 따라서 다르다 as it means the same thing.

Ex)

때에 따라 달라요.

= 때에 따라서 달라요.

상황에 따라 달라요.

= 상황에 따라서 달라요.

You can choose whichever structure you are more comfortable with saying. They are both correct.

-마다 다르다

-마다 means "every", so 아침마다 is "every morning", and 밤마다 is "every night". When you use -마다 with 다르다, it means "It is different for every…".

Ex)

사람마다

= every person

해마다

= every year

달마다

= every month

주말마다

= every weekend

Sample Sentences

사람마다 달라요.

= For every person, it is different.

= It depends on the person.

나라마다 달라요.

= It depends on the country.

해마다 달라요.

= It depends on the year.

= It is different every year.

Difference Between -에 따라 and -마다

These two phrases are usually interchangeable, but -마다 can only be used with nouns, whereas -에 따라 can also be used with a clause. In order for -에 따라 to be used with a clause, however, you need to conjugate the verb into the -는지 form.

Also, while -에 따라 has a stronger meaning of, "It depends on the certain item/circumstance", -마다 can also have the meaning that something constantly changes, even if it is not really "in accordance with" the item or circumstance.

For example, 해마다 달라요 can mean, "It depends on that year" or "It changes every year."

Verb Stem + -는지에 따라(서) 다르다

Sample Sentences

언제 가는지에 따라 달라요.

= It depends on when you go there.

어디서 사는지에 따라 달라요.

= It depends on where you buy it.

누구한테 이야기하는지에 따라서 달라요.

= It depends on whom you talk to.

-는지에 따라 = -느냐에 따라

Sometimes you will also hear people saying -느냐에 따라 instead of -는지에 따라. They are interchangeable, but -느냐에 따라 is slightly more commonly used in spoken Korean.

Ex)

언제 가는지에 따라 달라요.

= 언제 가느냐에 따라 달라요.

달라요 vs. 달라져요

You will also often hear people saying, "달라져요" instead of "달라요" to put stress on the nuance that it "becomes" different, but usually just saying "달라요" is clear enough.

Track 55

Sample Dialogue

손님: 머리 파마하려고 하는데요. 얼마예요?

미용사: 머리 길이에 따라 달라요.
단발머리니까 기본 가격으로 해
드릴게요.

손님: 이 스타일로 해 주세요.

미용사: 아! 손님, 이 머리는 파마한 머리가
아니에요. 고데기로 한 머리예요.

Customer: I want to get a perm. How much is it?

*Hairdresser: It depends on the length of the hair.
Since your hair is bobbed, I can do it for
the base price.*

Customer: Please do it in this style.

*Hairdresser: Ah! This hair isn't permed. This style
is done with a flat iron.*

✎ *Exercises for Lesson 28*

Translate each sentence into Korean by using -에 따라 달라요.

1. It depends on the person.

....

2. It depends on the situation.

....

3. It depends on the time.

....

4. It depends on when you go there.

....

5. It depends on where you buy it.

....

Check the answers on **p.211**

187

by Expressing Doubts, Abilities, and Happenings

LESSON 29

Sometimes I do this, but other times I do that.

Track 57

In this lesson, we are going to look at how to say, "Sometimes I do this, sometimes I do that" or "Sometimes it is like this, other times it is like that" in Korean.

In order to say this, there are a few things you need to know. First of all, you need to know how to use the -(으)ㄹ 때 ending, which means "when + Subject + Verb". You also need to know how the topic marker -는 is used to show contrast.

How to Say "sometimes" in Korean

When the word "sometimes" is used just to show the frequency of an action, you can say 가끔, 가끔씩, or 때때로. 가끔 and 가끔씩 are more common in spoken Korean than 때때로. 때때로 is very formal and used in written language.

When you want to literally say "sometimes" and "other times", you can use the expression, **어떨 때**. 어떨 때 comes from 어떻다 + -(으)ㄹ + 때.

어떻다 means "to be how" or "to be in what kind of state", -(으)ㄹ marks a future action or state, and 때 means "time" or "when". So literally, 어떨 때 means "when what state will happen" or "when things are how". Therefore, when more naturally translated, 어떨 때 means "in what kind of situation", "in what kind of times", or even just "when".

Ex)

어떨 때 영화 보고 싶어요?

= When do you (usually) feel like watching a movie?

어떨 때 제일 힘들어요?

= When do you (usually) have the hardest time?

As you can notice from the examples above, 어떨 때 is commonly used when you are asking about a general pattern or habit, whereas 언제 has a simpler meaning of "when".

Track 57

어떨 때 can also be used to mean "sometimes", but this is when you want to show contrast between "sometimes" and "other times". Therefore, you usually use 어떨 때 with the topic marker, -는.

어떨 때는 = sometimes + certain state/action

+

어떨 때는 = other times + another state/action

Like shown above, you can repeat 어떨 때는. Let's take a look at some examples.

Ex)

커피요? 어떨 때는 마시는데, 어떨 때는 안 마셔요.

= Coffee? Sometimes I drink it, but other times, I do not drink it.

189

어떨 때는 혼자 있는 것이 좋은데, 어떨 때는 싫어요.

= Sometimes I like being alone, but other times, I do not like it.

If you want to be more specific and say "other times" in Korean as well, you can use the expression 다른 때는 with the verb 다르다; however, 어떨 때는 is used more than 다른 때는 (Although 어떨 때는 is more commonly used, some people also use 어떤 때는, since it is in the present tense).

Sample Sentences

그 사람은 어떨 때는 친절한데, 어떨 때는 정말 불친절해요.

= Sometimes he is kind, but other times, he is very unkind.

어떨 때는 일을 그만두고 싶은데, 어떨 때는 일하는 게 좋아요.

= Sometimes I feel like quitting my job, but other times, I like working.

Track 57

You can also use the ending -(으)ㄹ 때도 있어요 after the second 어떨 때는 clause. For example, the above sentence can be changed to, "어떨 때는 일을 그만두고 싶은데, 어떨 때는 일 하는 게 좋을 때도 있어요."

-(으)ㄹ 때 means "a time when…" and -도 있어요 means "There are also…". Therefore, this is to express the meaning "There are also times when…".

Ex)

어떨 때는 운동하는 게 재미있는데, 어떨 때는 운동하고 싶지 않을 때도 있어요.

= Sometimes working out is fun, but other times, there are also times when I do not feel like doing exercise.

You can also make this shorter.

어떨 때는 운동하는 게 재미있는데, 운동하고 싶지 않을 때도 있어요.

어떨 때는 운동하는 게 재미있는데, 어떨 때는 운동하고 싶지 않아요.

Track 57

by Expressing Doubts, Abilities, and Happenings

Sample Dialogue

Track 58

환자: 안녕하세요, 의사 선생님. 제가 코를 너무 심하게 골아서 왔어요.

의사: 매일 밤 골아요?

환자: 아니요. 어떨 때는 심하게 고는데, 어떨 때는 안 골 때도 있어요.

Patient: Hello, Doctor. I came because I have trouble with severe snoring.

Doctor: Do you snore every night?

Patient: No. Sometimes I snore heavily, but there are times when I don't snore at all.

✏ Exercises for Lesson **29**

Translate each sentence into Korean and write it on the lines provided.

1. Sometimes I drink it, but other times, I do not drink it.

....

2. Sometimes I like being alone, but other times, I do not like it.

....

3. Sometimes he is kind, but other times, he is very unkind.

....

4. Sometimes I feel like quitting my job, but other times, I like working.

....

Check the answers on **p.211**

193

by Expressing Doubts, Abilities, and Happenings

LESSON **30**

Sentence Building Drill 8

Sentence Building Drill 8

In this series, we focus on how you can use the grammatical rules and expressions that you have learned so far to train yourself to comfortably and flexibly make more Korean sentences.

We will start off with THREE key sentences, then practice changing parts of these sentences so that you do not end up just memorizing the same three sentences. We want you to be able to be as flexible as possible with the Korean sentences that you can make.

Key Sentence (1)

별로 안 어려울 줄 알았는데 생각보다 어려웠어요.

= I thought it would not be so difficult, but it was more difficult than I had thought.

Key Sentence (2)

그 사람 알기는 아는데 자주 안 만나는 편이에요.

= I DO know him, but I do not really meet him often.

Key Sentence (3)

제 이름은 발음하기가 어려워서 잊어버리기 쉬워요.

= My name is difficult to pronounce, so it is easy to forget.

Expansion & Variation Practice with Key Sentence (1)

0. Original sentence:

별로 안 어려울 줄 알았는데 생각보다 어려웠어요.

= I thought it would not be so difficult, but it was more difficult than I had thought.

1.

별로 안 어려울 줄 알았는데 = I thought it would not be so difficult, but...

아무도 없을 줄 알았는데 = I thought nobody would be here, but...

여기에 있을 줄 알았는데 = I thought it would be here, but...

괜찮을 줄 알았는데 = I thought it would be okay, but...

Track 59

2.

생각보다 어려웠어요. = it was more difficult than I thought.

생각보다 빨리 끝났어요. = it finished earlier than I thought.

생각보다 간단했어요. = it was simpler than I thought.

생각보다 비쌀 수도 있어요. = it might be more expensive than you think.

Expansion & Variation Practice with Key Sentence (2)

0. Original sentence:

그 사람 알기는 아는데 자주 안 만나는 편이에요.

= I DO know him, but I do not really meet him often.

195

1.

그 사람 알기는 아는데 = I DO know him, but...

이거 좋기는 좋은데 = This IS good, but...

비싸기는 비싼데 = It IS expensive, but...

하기는 할 건데 = I AM going to do it, but...

2.

자주 안 만나는 *편이에요. = I do not really meet him often.

별로 안 좋아하는 편이에요. = I do not really like it.

다른 사람들보다는** 잘하는 편이에요. = I am rather good at it, compared to other people.

가끔씩 가는 편이에요. = I go there sometimes.

* 편이다 shows a tendency to do/not do a trend or habit. By adding 편이다 you are being a little more indirect.

** We added -는 to show contrast.

Track
59

Expansion & Variation Practice with Key Sentence (3)

0. Original sentence:

제 이름은 발음하기가 어려워서 잊어버리기 쉬워요.

= My name is difficult to pronounce, so it is easy to forget.

1.

제 이름은 발음하기가 어려워요.

= My name is difficult to pronounce.

이건 혼자서 만들기가 어려워요.

= This is difficult to make by yourself.

196

지도가 복잡해서 찾아 가기 어려워요.

= The map is complicated so it is difficult to find the place.

한국어는 배우기 어렵지 않아요.

= Korean is not difficult to learn.

2.

잊어버리기 쉬워요. = It is easy to forget.

실수하기 쉬워요. = It is easy to make a mistake.

포기하기 쉬워요. = It is easy to give up.

찾기 쉬워요. = It is easy to find.

Track
59

by Expressing Doubts, Abilities, and Happenings

Sample Dialogue

Track 60

경은: 영화 재미있었어요?

주연: 재미있을 줄 알았는데 생각보다 재미없었어요.

경은: 왜요?

주연: 좀 이해하기 어려웠거든요.

Kyeong-eun: Was the movie good?

Jooyeon: I thought it would be, but it wasn't as good as I thought.

Kyeong-eun: Why?

Jooyeon: Because it was kind of difficult to understand.

✏ Exercises for Lesson *30*

Translate each phrase or sentence into Korean and then write it on the lines provided below.

1. It is easy to forget.

....

2. I thought it would be okay, but...

....

3. It was more difficult than I thought.

....

4. I do not really like it.

....

5. My name is difficult to pronounce.

....

Check the answers on **p.211**

199

by Expressing Doubts, Abilities, and Happenings

BLOG

Johnny's Korean Movie Recommendations

I'm a huge fan of movies. I typically try to watch at least one per week. Let's be honest though, I probably watch around 4 movies every week. Some are fantastic, some are okay, and then some are just straight up bad. I enjoy just about every genre as well and try to keep up with movies from around the world.

If you don't know, but I'm sure you already do, Korea makes some amazing films. Some of my favorite movies are Korean movies. There is something about the style of a good Korean film that I just absolutely love. Therefore, I'd like to go through some of my favorite Korean films.

* These are in no particular order.

#5. 과속 스캔들 (Scandal Makers) 2008

Let's start off with some light fun. This movie follows Nam Hyeon-Soo, a radio host played by Cha Tae-Hyun, as he finds out he has a daughter and a grandson. His daughter, played by Park Bo-Young, blackmails him into letting them stay at his house. They begin living with each other but since their ages are not too far apart and they both look young, people begin to think they are romantically involved. The movie is full of laughs but at times can get quite serious as it touches on some tough issues. The grandson is played by Wang Seok-Hyeon and was absolutely fantastic in the role. Whenever he is on screen, it is almost impossible not to smile at how cute he is. If you like comedies that don't mind touching on serious issues, I think *Scandal Makers* is for you.

#4. 좋은 놈, 나쁜 놈, 이상한 놈 (The Good, the Bad, and the Weird) 2008

Moving on with a bit of action, *The Good, the Bad, and the Weird* still keeps it light. I'm a huge fan of western movies, and one of my favorite movies of all time is *The Good, the Bad, and the Ugly*, a Spaghetti Western. The Korean version isn't a straight remake of the original as it brings a lot of originality to the screen. The film stars Lee Byung-Hun, Song Kang-Ho, and Jung Woo-Sung, who are some of my favorite Korean actors. From the beginning to the end, this movie is a fun ride. All three actors bring a great performance that stands apart from the rest. If you like action movies, this is a must-see. The scale is big and there is even a bit of Mad Max thrown in there as well.

#3. 곡성 (The Wailing) 2016

This is a horror film. I know a lot of people don't really like horror films, but if you can watch them, I'd watch this one. It stars Kwak Do-Won, Hwang Jung-Min, and Chun Woo-Hee. This was Kwak Do-Won's first time in a lead role, and he was perfect for it! The film follows a police officer played by Do-Won who is investigating the cause of a series of murders occurring in a small village. The movie has so many twists and turns that it will keep you guessing until the very end. You won't know who to trust until it is too late. If you do end up watching this movie, maybe try watching it during the daytime with all of your lights on. Once the movie ends, you may not want to sleep for a few hours.

#2. 아는 여자 (Someone Special) 2004

After the last movie, I can sense that some of you are feeling a bit uneasy, so let's jump to a light romantic comedy. I enjoy a good romantic comedy now and again, and *Someone Special* is one of the good ones. *Someone Special*, or the literal translation, A Woman I Know, follows a struggling baseball player played by Jung Jae-Young. At the start of the movie, his girlfriend breaks up with him and he finds out he only has 3 months to live after visiting the doctor. Now some of you are probably asking, "But wait, you said this was a romantic comedy. How can this be a comedy if it's about a man who is about to die in 3 months?" Well, it's all the stuff that happens in those three months that makes this movie fun. One of the things I really liked about this movie was how it pokes fun at some of the tropes you typically see in romantic comedies. That, added with a great performance by Lee Na-Young, makes *Someone Special* a movie to watch.

#1. 괴물 (The Host) 2006

I'm a sucker for monster movies, and Korea did a fantastic job with *The Host* (literal translation Monster). *The Host* follows Park Gang-Du, played by Song Kang-Ho, as he tries to rescue his daughter after being kidnapped by a monster from the Han River. I absolutely loved how this movie didn't take itself too seriously. Even though it is a monster movie, they keep it light so just about anyone can enjoy it. The movie will have you laughing at parts but also on the edge of your seat at other points in the film. *The Host* also stars Bae Doo-Na. This movie became Korea's highest grossing movie at the time and went on to win several awards including Best Film at the Asian Film Awards.

I wish I could go on about other movies but there just aren't enough pages in this book to go over all of the films I like. I hope this gives you a good starting point if you have been wondering which Korean movies to watch.

* Oh! And here is a tip for you. Some theaters have this really cool photo ticket that you can make. If you do decide to watch a movie during your stay in Korea, I highly suggest getting at least one. It makes for a great souvenir to take back home. I've been collecting them since they started and will make a poster of all the movies I've watched over the past several years.

If you are thinking of getting a photo ticket, you have to download a cinema app, such as CGV or Lotte Cinema, and make a reservation for the movie you want to see through the app. After you have made your reservation, you will need to find a poster or a photo that you would like to use for your photo ticket. You can use just about any photo; it doesn't even have to be the movie poster if you don't want to go that route! When you get to the theater, there will be a photo ticket kiosk where you can print out your photo ticket. Just follow the instructions on the screen and there you go! You have your very own photo ticket to remember the day when you watched that particular film. Don't worry even if you forgot to print out the photo ticket on the day you watched the movie. You can do it within one to two months, depending on the cinema.

Written by Johnny Bland

You've finished Level 6! 축하합니다!!

ANSWERS

for Level 6, Lessons 1 ~ 30

Answers for Level 6, Lesson 1

1. 이거 어때요? = How about this?

2. 내일 어때요? = How about tomorrow?

3. 다시 하는 거 어때요? = How about doing it again?

4. 내일 만나서 이야기하는 거 어때요? = How about meeting and talking about it tomorrow?

5. 이렇게 하는 게 어때요? = How about doing it this way?

6. 이렇게 하는 건 어때요? = (Since you are not too sure about the other ideas,) How about doing it THIS way (then)?

Answers for Level 6, Lesson 2

1. 학교 어떤 것 같아요?

2. 물어보는 것 어떤 것 같아요? or 물어보는 거 어떤 것 같아요?

3. 이 책 어떤 것 같아요?

4. 어릴 때 유학 가는 것 어떤 것 같아요? or 어릴 때 유학 가는 거 어떤 것 같아요?

5. 제 아이디어 어떤 것 같아요?

Answers for Level 6, Lesson 3

1. 가장 빠른 길 중 하나

2. 가장 자주 만나는 친구 중 한 명

3. 가장 좋아하는 가수들 중 한 명

4. 제일 자주 오는 카페 중 하나

5. 가장 인기 있는 영화 중 하나

Answers for Level 6, Lesson 4

1. - (저) 여기 앉아도 돼요?

- (저) 여기 앉아도 괜찮아요?

- (저) 여기 앉아도 될까요?

2. - 창문 닫아도 돼요?

- 창문 닫아도 괜찮아요?

- 창문 닫아도 될까요?

3. - 나중에 (or 이따가) 전화해도 돼요?

- 나중에 (or 이따가) 전화해도 괜찮아요?

- 나중에 (or 이따가) 전화해도 될까요?

4. - (저) 먼저 가도 돼요?

- (저) 먼저 가도 괜찮아요?

- (저) 먼저 가도 될까요?

5. - 이거 열어 봐도 돼요?

- 이거 열어 봐도 괜찮아요?

- 이거 열어 봐도 될까요?

Answers for Level 6, Lesson 5

1. 가고 있는 중이에요. (가는 중이에요. is also possible.)

2. 뭐 하고 있는 중이에요? (뭐 하는 중이에요? is also possible.)

3. 뭐 하고 있는 중이었어요? (뭐 하는 중이었어요? is also possible.)

4. 열쇠를 찾고 있는 중이었어요. (열쇠를 찾는 중이었어요. is also possible.)

5. 아직 고르고 있는 중이에요. (아직 고르는 중이에요. is also possible.)

Answers for Level 6, Lesson 6

1. 의사 선생님

2. 교수님

3. 손님

4. 어머님

Answers for Level 6, Lesson 7

Examples answers:

1. 어차피 다시 올 거예요.

2. 어차피 늦었으니까 천천히 와. (This is something you can only say to your close friend with whom you use casual language, so it is in 반말 form.)

3. 어차피 제가 할 수 있는 일이 아니에요.

4. 어차피 해야 되는 거니까, 재미있게 해요.

Answers for Level 6, Lesson 8

1. 이거 누구 책인지 잘 모르겠어요.

2. 서점이 내일 문을 열지 잘 모르겠어요. (서점이 내일 문을 열 건지 잘 모르겠어요. is also possible.)

3. 다 끝났는지 잘 모르겠어요.

4. 이게 무슨 뜻인지 잘 모르겠어요.

5. 내일 만날지 안 만날지 잘 모르겠어요.

Answers for Level 6, Lesson 9

1. 도서관에 가는 김에

2. 말이 나온 김에

3. 서울에 온 김에

4. 시작한 김에

Answers for Level 6, Lesson 10

1. 일하는 중이에요. (일하고 있는 중이에요. is also possible.)

2. 우리 어차피 늦을 거예요.

3. 오늘 바쁘니까 내일 만나요.

4. 다음에 갈까요?

5. 제가 제일 자주 만나는 친구들 중 한 명이에요.

Answers for Level 6, Lesson 11

1. 준다고요

2. 간다는 말이에요 (거기에 간다고요 is also possible.)

3. 아니

4. 제 말은

Answers for Level 6, Lesson 12

1. What do you mean?, What is that supposed to mean?, What does that mean?, or What are you talking about?

2. 무슨 소리예요?

3. 말씀

4. 무슨 말씀이세요?

5. 무슨 뜻이에요?

Answers for Level 6, Lesson 13

1. 과 (過)

2. 과식 (過食)

3. 과속 (過速)

4. 과로 (過勞)

5. 과정 (過程)

Answers for Level 6, Lesson 14

1. 쓸 겸

2. 할 겸

3. 할 겸, 찍을 겸

4. 살 겸, 볼 겸

Answers for Level 6, Lesson 15

1. 부자라는 것은 (부자란 is also possible.)

2. 자유라는 것은 (자유란 is also possible.)

3. 우정이라는 것은 (우정이란 is also possible.)

4. 꿈이라는 것은 (꿈이란 is also possible.)

Answers for Level 6, Lesson 16

1. 아프겠어요.

2. 이게 좋겠어요.

3. 이러다가 늦겠어요.

4. 힘들어 죽겠어요.

Answers for Level 6, Lesson 17

1. 내일은 안 바빠요. 오늘 일을 다 끝냈거든요.

2. 아직 말할 수 없어요. 비밀이거든요.

3. 이따가 전화할게요. 제가 지금 좀 바쁘거든요.

4. 제가 지금 돈이 없거든요. 만 원만 빌려주세요.

Answers for Level 6, Lesson 18

1. 이나

2. 이나

3. 가거나

4. 아니면

Answers for Level 6, Lesson 19

1. 달라졌어요

2. 달라진

3. 없어졌어요

4. 많아졌어요

5. 좋아졌어요

Answers for Level 6, Lesson 20

Suggested answers:

1. 그러니까 이거 뭐예요?

2. 누구하고 같이 갈 거라고요?

3. 아니면 다른 사람에게 부탁할게요.

4. 제 친구가 알 수도 있어요.

5. 인사도 할 겸

Answers for Level 6, Lesson 21

1. 이용되다 (이용되어지다 is also possible.)

2. 보내지다

3. 먹히다

4. 잡히다

5. 풀리다 (풀어지다 is also possible.)

Answers for Level 6, Lesson 22

1. 무 (無)

2. 무죄 (無罪)

3. 무인 (無人)

4. 무능력 (無能力)

5. 무책임 (無責任)

Answers for Level 6, Lesson 23

1. 안 만들어져요

2. 안 잘라져요

3. 안 들려요

4. 안 보여요

5. 안 돼요

Answers for Level 6, Lesson 24

I. 맛있기는 맛있는데, 좀 짜요. or 맛있기는 한데, 좀 짜요.

2. 좋기는 좋은데, 너무 비싸요. or 좋기는 한데, 너무 비싸요.

3. 보기는 봤는데 기억이 안 나요. or 보기는 했는데 기억이 안 나요.

4. 읽기는 읽었는데 이해가 안 돼요. or 읽기는 했는데 이해가 안 돼요.

5. 어제 친구를 만나기는 했는데, 금방 헤어졌어요. or 어제 친구를 만나기는 만났는데, 금방 헤어졌어요.

Answers for Level 6, Lesson 25

I. 사용하기(가/에) 쉬워요.

2. 이건 만들기(가) 어려워요.

3. 이건 어린이가 사용하기(에) 어려워요.

4. 제 이름은 발음하기(가) 어려워요.

Answers for Level 6, Lesson 26

I. 이게 여기 있을 줄 몰랐어요.

2. (저는) 경화 씨도 온 줄 알았어요.

3. (저는) 안 어려울 줄 알았어요.

4. 제가 뭐라고 말할 줄 알았어요?

5. 이렇게 비싼 줄 몰랐어요.

Answers for Level 6, Lesson 27

I. 운전 할 줄 알아요?

2. 자전거 탈 줄 알아요?

3. 이거 할 줄 알아요?

4. 김치 만들 줄 알아요?

5. 한국어로 말할 줄 알아요?

Answers for Level 6, Lesson 28

I. 사람에 따라 달라요.

2. 상황에 따라 달라요.

3. 때에 따라 달라요. (시간에 따라 달라요. is also possible.)

4. 언제 가는지에 따라 달라요. or 언제 가느냐에 따라 달라요.

5. 어디서 사는지에 따라 달라요. or 어디서 사느냐에 따라 달라요.

Answers for Level 6, Lesson 29

Suggested answers:

I. 어떨 때는 마시는데, 어떨 때는 안 마셔요.

2. 어떨 때는 혼자 있는 것이 좋은데, 어떨 때는 싫어요.

3. 그 사람은 어떨 때는 친절한데, 어떨 때는 정말 불친절해요.

4. 어떨 때는 일을 그만두고 싶은데, 어떨 때는 일 하는 게 좋아요.

Answers for Level 6, Lesson 30

I. 잊어버리기 쉬워요.

2. 괜찮을 줄 알았는데

3. 생각보다 어려웠어요.

4. 별로 안 좋아하는 편이에요.

5. 제 이름은 발음하기가 어려워요.

Notes On Using This Book

Colored Text

Colored text indicates that there is an accompanying audio file. You can download the MP3 audio files at **https://talktomeinkorean.com/audio**.

Hyphen

Some grammar points have a hyphen attached at the beginning, such as -이/가, -(으)ㄹ 거예요, -(으)려고 하다, and -은/는커녕. This means that the grammar point is dependent, so it needs to be attached to another word such as a noun, a verb, or a particle.

Parentheses

When a grammar point includes parentheses, such as -(으)ㄹ 거예요 or (이)랑, this means that the part in the parentheses can be omitted depending on the word it is attached to.

Slash

When a grammar point has a slash, such as -아/어/여서 or -은/는커녕, this means that only one of the syllables before or after the slash can be used at a time. In other words, -은/는커녕 is used as either -은커녕 or -는커녕, depending on the word it is attached to.

Descriptive Verb

In TTMIK lessons, adjectives in English are referred to as "descriptive verbs" because they can be conjugated as verbs depending on the tense.